FIFTEEN PAST SEVENTY
Counsel from My Elders

James Maas

SHAMELESS HUSSY PRESS   BERKELEY

Drawings by Fran Raboff

Published in 1980 in the United States of America
by SHAMELESS HUSSY PRESS
  Box 3092
  Berkeley, California 94703

ISBN 0-915288-42-7

Printed and bound in the United States of America

Contents

Contents

Preface

FIFTEEN PAST SEVENTY is a book whose focus is the interviews I had with fifteen vital people in their seventies and eighties. The words are theirs, and the book is *about* them. It is not a book *for* them or for any other older people. It is not a book about the problems and processes of aging. It doesn't give advice on how to stay young, and it has nothing to do with the rights of Senior Citizens.

It is a book about being alive and enjoying life, and it is told by people who have retained their zest for life regardless of their chronological age, the amount of money they have to live on, or, as I was to find, the state of their health. It is about the kind of old age I'd like for myself. It is written for me and the people like me who have been unwilling to accept their middle years because they have been afraid of facing their older years.

Prologue

Shortly after my 57th birthday, my friend Giovanni died a lingering, pain-filled death from the effects of his coronary bypass surgery a year or two earlier and from the cancer that destroyed his liver just before he turned 80. I saw him twice during the last month of his life. On the Saturday before the end, I was shaken by the newly-sunken cheeks and eyes. He was asleep while I sat by his bed, holding his hand, and he stirred only when Gail, his wife, said to him loudly, "Giovanni, Jim is here to see you." The ever-so-faint smile that curled the corners of his mouth was recognition enough . . . was last contact enough . . . from a man whom I loved.

Giovanni was other people to me besides a friend. He was a battler, forced on to crutches by polio at the age of three, who had gone on to win fencing championships as an adult. He was an artist who saw artistry in everyone and art in everything around him. He was a teacher who helped his students examine their own creations. And he was, for me, the model of what a father ought to be to his sons . . . caring, energetic, helpful, knowledgeable, versatile . . . you know the fantasy well, I'm sure. All these people I lost when Giovanni died, and I grieved his death.

His dying put me back in touch with a host of well-covered-over fears about my getting old and my death. His suffering, his dying in pain, barely able to recognize the voices of people who loved him or the hands that held his, triggered off powerful feelings. That was not the way I wanted to die!

From the time I accepted, as a young teenager, that it really was possible that I might die some day, I have had a deep-seated fear of growing old and dying. Even the idea of looking at a corpse was enough to terrify me. I wouldn't go to movies in which I knew a body was going to fall out of a closet, and if, by mistake, I went to one and the body did fall out, I would quickly cover my eyes. I couldn't look into the casket to see my father after he died when I was 30 and I couldn't go out into the street to pick up the intact body of our dead dog when I was 45.

Almost as pervasive in my 50's has been the fear of incapacitating illness and pain when I get old. I dreaded becoming a "vegetable." I fought the notion of retirement at 65. I joined the American Association of Retired People to see what their travel packages were like, but I snickered at the old folks being herded on and off buses when I saw their tours to the vacation spots that my wife and I were visiting on our own. And I certainly did not read their monthly magazine.

I remember cringing inside when I interviewed for a job at one of the better-run homes for the aged in San Francisco. I had the creepy feeling of being in a place where old parents were sent to die. Within a few minutes after my interview with the director of the home started, I heard myself describing the residents I had seen in the lobby as "inmates." I was relieved that I didn't get the job and that the interview was short.

And here I was at 57, still having trouble thinking of myself as middle-aged. I was still playing basketball with men much younger than I . . . in some cases a third my age . . . partly for the sheer enjoyment, partly to keep in physical trim, but mostly to assure myself that I was still young. After all, how many guys do you know who are still playing basketball at that age? How sweet it was when people on the court or at the office expressed surprise when they heard I was 57. "Why, you don't look much older than 40 or 45," they said, and I glowed.

And then there was the pride I took in being the oldest student in my Master's program at Cal. In retrospect it seems just another way of reassuring myself that I was as productive as all those younger students . . . and what's more, I had the grade point average to prove it. Older, yes, but middle-aged, no!

And yet my body was telling me differently. There were the low back pains, the cuts and scratches that took longer to heal, the sore Achilles tendons, the eyeglass prescriptions that needed changing, and all the other little signals that you know about as well as I do. So, slowly and reluctantly, I began to accept that I was indeed 57 and maybe middle aged. But old? No way! I was not old! I would not stop working at age 65. I would not give up sex or basketball or backpacking. I didn't want to sit in a chair watching TV all day. I didn't want to be one of those bent old people inching their way across a pedestrian zone on a busy street. I didn't want to become a financial drain on my family. I didn't want to vegetate in a "convalescent home." I didn't want to linger on and die in pain like Giovanni.

A month or two after Giovanni died, I read a book by Joyce Stephens called *Loners, Losers and Lovers*, in which there is a description of an SRO . . . a single room occupancy hotel which had

> two public restrooms (shower and commode) on each floor, one for men and one for women. . . . The units have neither cooking facilities nor refrigerators. All rooms contain a bed, wash basin, a dresser, and a chair. The furniture is cheap and generally in need of repair. Paint is peeling off the walls, and cockroaches are abundant. During the winter months, rooms above the fourth floor are inadequately heated. The halls are dimly lit. . . ."

Only one small particular . . . a naked light bulb hanging from the ceiling . . . separated that SRO from earlier fantasies for my own old age.

By the time I finished the book, something new happened inside me. I became aware how much time I had spent thinking about the "loners" and the "losers," and avoiding the "lovers" . . . the winners. The truth is tht I have known many, many winners. My mother is a vivacious 86, still dressing like a million dollars and still looking at least 15 years younger than she is. My Aunt Sarah, well over 80, still writes children's books. A friend's grandmother, who died at 104, was 96 and baking apple pies in her own kitchen for the family Thanksgiving dinner when I last saw her. I had plenty of heroes like Charlie Chaplin and George Bernard Shaw, whom I idolized as much for their energy in their later years as for their wit and wisdom. Theirs was the kind of old age I wanted. When I was young, I dreamed about living until I was 80, so that I could see the year 2000 come in. It's the same dream now that I'm only a little over 20 years away from it, but with a different twist to it. . . . I want to be as energetic and productive as those winners when I get there.

I decided I needed to find a number of energetic older people . . . the "lovers" . . . to listen to. I wanted to hear them tell me what their lives were like, and I wanted to discover what it was about them that was different than the "loners" and the "losers." Was it something about their genetic make-up, their childhood experience, their relationships with the opposite sex, their level of health, their diet and physical activity, their occupations, their incomes, their religious faith? Was there a common theme in their lives . . . some panacea . . . some unique piece of wisdom they owned that would help reassure me that being old is not necessarily bad . . . that there might even be some advantage to old age. I think, on some level, I must have recognized that the panacea doesn't exist . . . but no matter, it was an exploration I had to pursue.

I deliberately excluded the people who seem to be putting in time . . . sitting in front of television sets in downtown hotel lobbies, or having dinner by themselves night after night in some neighborhood cafeteria. I selected only the people who have so much living yet to do. It was unscientific and unfair, I know, to lump all older people into either "putting-in-time" or "so-much-living-yet-to-do" categories, but the way for me to make peace with old age was to ignore my long held fears of it and listen to the voices of people who were enjoying theirs. I did just that, and I later wrote this book around the interviews with fifteen of them.

I am quite sure I could have found a lot of the "putting-in-time" people to interview, but I was not at all sure how to go about finding the people I really wanted to listen to. To my surprise, I discovered that whenever I told friends what I was doing, almost every one of them knew some wonderful older person that "you absolutely must talk to." They were helpful in arranging introductions for me, and I was successful in getting an interview with every person to whom I was introduced.

Although it was marvelously reassuring to know that there are so many people who are willing to help me and whose lives match my vision of what I want my old age to be like, I was not completely at ease stepping into the lives of people whom I had not met before. I needn't have worried. The interviews turned out to be delightful, warming experiences. The structured outline of questions I had prepared, I scarcely used. I just asked what seemed important to me at the moment, and the responses flowed back easily to me. After the interviews, I could hardly wait to get home to share the experience with my wife and to listen again to the beautiful words I had captured on tape. Those were heady days.

I believe the enjoyment of the interviews was mutual. I was told many times how nice it felt to be chosen for an interview, and how much fun it was to reminisce about long-forgotten events. Not everyone understood my need to interview him, but each one was interested in what I was doing, and wanted to help.

One final note: I deliberately changed the names of the people and most of the place names. I changed them reluctantly, because I wish that you had the opportunity of looking up phone numbers and having chats with "my" Fifteen, but I decided that it was more important to keep their identities private.

Acknowledgments

My role in this production was in many ways like that of a host on a radio or television talk show. I was center stage, but I was also very dependent on the people behind the scenes and on the guest performers.

The backstage people were Marjorie Simon, mother, who has long encouraged me to write; Lucile Lockhart, colleague, who helped shape the ideas; Henrik Blum, teacher, who helped me understand what I could accomplish; and, most importantly, Helen Maas, wife, who seemingly never tired of hearing me ask, "Holly, would you listen to this for just a minute?" There were many others in the crew: Barbara Weiss, Mel Krantzler, Lucille Burlew-Lawler, Bill Mandel . . . who helped polish the production. To all of them . . . thank you, thank you. *I* know it was not a one-man show.

The fifteen guests, a portion of whose lives appear on these pages, were the real stars. To say thank you to them for their openness, their warmth, their time, and their encouragement seems so inadequate, but I don't know how to express it better. I hope they know how much richer I am for having known them.

1

I Always Try to Live
so I Don't Hurt Nobody

*(William Eckhardt is an 89 year old man who
has farmed in South Dakota most of his life.
He was born on the farm that his mother and
father homesteaded. He now lives in a one-
bedroom apartment in downtown Oakland.
The walls are ablaze with color.)*

One afternoon, about four o'clock, my mother was tending chickens, and we kids were with her. And the sky was just hanging . . . full of black clouds and they have lightning in them. Then mother said, "Children, better get in the house. Maybe it's gonna start to rain anytime." And so I started out . . . you see on the farm, between the house and the barn is usually a barbed wire fence and a narrow gate . . . and I betcha I wasn't six feet from the gate post, and the lightning struck the gate post. I remember I was all fire, but I didn't hear the crack anymore. I was unconscious about five hours. That was in South Dakota . . . about five miles from a little bitty town. You see, my folks were pioneers. They came and homesteaded and they got 160 acre of land. . . . But my brains was damaged and my memory is no good. . . .

I was married in '15 and I took over my father's farm in '16. And then in '46, my son took over, and we moved into that little town near the farm. My wife was also a German. And then . . . let's see . . . that was in '14, late in the fall, and my folks was invited to a Hungarian wedding. They did some dancing. The room was about this size. And they have beer and Hungarian paprikash . . . that was pretty hot stuff. And that way I meet her and she start to be my girl. And on the 24th of June, in '15, we were married. And we have five children. The oldest was born in July, '16, and the girl was next in '20. And then the daughter here in Oakland in '25. And another daughter in '29. And then in '33 another boy sneaked in.

Ya, I had good wife. At first she didn't know a word of English. We always talked German all the time, but she could later talk English about as good as I could. So, many of the folks we get acquainted with were German. I like folks that are straight. They don't have to act religious, just so they love their neighbor. I always try to live so I don't hurt nobody. They all be my neighbors. I always get along. I never were in trouble. Ya, I guess that's important . . . to live right. Treat them right and they treat you right. If I sold something, it had to be good, otherwise I wouldn't sell it.

When I farmed I didn't miss college, but I do now more than ever. . . . If I could finish 8th grade or high school . . . because I can read, but not good enough to enjoy it. I miss words. I could entertain or visit better with people and talk better with them. My English . . . it's just everyday talk . . . I don't know enough words. So I do needlepoint, like these coasters. I finish them and I give them away. All these here I give to the Senior Center. I gave them 12 already. And then I have two cousins that I give to. My daughter likes them too. . . . You see the jigsaw puzzles on walls? I have thick cardboard and I do jigsaw puzzles by the window in the morning and afternoon. In the evening I do needlepoint work. And my daughter always gets the hometown newspaper and brings it to me, and I read that.

I get the Social Security, but small. . . . I guess about $75. But on the farm I did pretty good, so I saved for the rainy day, ya. Now, I got it all borrowed out. My daughter takes care of everything . . . she borrowed it out. My rent is $175, and I do my own cooking. Very seldom I go out. So it don't cost much, and I'm already ahead $700 this year. . . . I never drawed on my principal. I get my interest every quarter right into my checking account. I feel comfortable. I like my apartment . . . with flowers. I only have four live plants now and two imitations, but I had 30 pots already two years ago. But I cut that down . . . too much waste.

I have color TV, but mostly I play the radio. It plays nice sound. And record player. . . . I don't have any friends, but my son in San Mateo comes to take me out once in awhile. My daughter lives here in Oakland and she eats with me about once a week . . . sometimes twice a week. I love to cook dinner. I cook beef stew . . . with onions . . . carrots . . . celery. I brown the meat and then after awhile I pressure cook it. After about 10 minutes, it's soft. My grandson was here about three weeks ago and he stayed for dinner. We had early dinner . . . about five o'clock . . . and he loved it! He had four helpings, and I enjoyed it because he liked it. . . .

On Saturday night I watch Lawrence Welk on TV. He has a nice program . . . a clean program . . . good music and good singing. I enjoy that Wheel of Fortune program, but that comes on at 10:30 in the morning, but 10:30 I should be down at Senior Center, otherwise I don't get no lunch. So I don't watch it any more. But the radio I have going quite a bit. I sit here and work with needlepoint. I do this wall hanging here. It belongs to my grandson, but he moved and we keep it here till he has a decent place. I made for a lady that my daughter knows a latch-hook rug 30 inches wide by five feet long for her office. And also for the same lady a floor pillow 23 inches by 23. I learned from my wife. Years ago I used to do fancy needlepoint with her . . . during the winter months.

I get up around seven in the morning . . . sometimes a little earlier. I fix my breakfast, and sometimes I work on a jigsaw puzzle. Then I wash up and shave and get all ready. Then it's 9:20 and I start out. You see, they open at nine o'clock at the Senior Center, and they start to sell meal tickets for lunch at 10 o'clock, and if you're not there, sometimes they're gone right away. So I get there about 20 minutes to ten and I get in the line right away. And until noon, I play cards . . . play hearts most of the time. After lunch, I play a game or two. But 1:30 or 2:00 I go home. On Wednesday they have movies . . . three movies and they usually last till 3:30 . . . sometimes a little later. And then I fool around a little . . . fix dinner . . . do needlepoint . . . and by 9:30 I go to bed. I don't sleep through. I have to get up about three or four times on account of pass water. My water bladder shrunk.

It's only a week I had the stomach flue for a day. Threw up. Monday I feel alright. I feel good otherwise. You see, I walk three and a half blocks to the Senior Center every day. Only my legs are weak . . . arthritis . . . a little pain. But I have to keep that up. I enjoy it too, because the weather's so nice out here. Sunshine, sunshine and no 40° below. . . .

I did some travelling. In Germany two times . . . in '30 by boat . . . in '70 by plane. And I was in Japan for 10 days in '71. Guatemala in '73. Oh ya . . . in '71 also a bus trip all over the United States. You see, my daughter works for a travel company and she can take two or three family once a year very cheap. I was in Hawaii three times. . . .

In '75 I sold my house and moved here. I'm here now for three years. The 28th of September it was three years. The first time I was here was in '58, and then we came out here every other year . . . sometimes six months here and six months back in South Dakota. And in '65 we had our Golden Wedding. After that my wife was mostly on the sick side. She had hardening of the arteries . . . no pain . . . lots of sleeping. She died in '68 . . . 72½ years old. She was not old and not young.

In a way, I was kinda glad she was relieved. She was so tired. Sometimes she slept about 18 hours. She was in the hospital in South Dakota for about 10 weeks, and when she got home she got weaker and weaker, and she was so weak when she sit up in in bed, she couldn't keep her balance. She falls over like a potato sack. So I made a frame out of this copper piping and hooked it into the mattress around back. Then I also put a pillow in back and then she could sit alright. I fixed her supper and brought it in and put a tray up for her and did everything . . . cut food up so she could eat everything with a spoon. She would eat everything and then she said I could go and eat my supper in the kitchen. One time, after awhile I went back to see how she was getting along, and the spoon was in her left hand. I said, "Mama, did you fall asleep?" And she didn't say nothing. And then I noticed she had a stroke, but she was still living.

So I called the doctor and the children. My oldest daughter stayed with me that night. And then later we all went to bed . . . we always slept in one bed, only she always slept on the left side on account of her heart. I was pretty tired and I fell asleep. Then later my daughter came in and checked on us about 11 o'clock, and she said to me, "Mom is dead."

I'm lonely but I get along. I always feel satisfied with myself. I know she was a good wife. We never have argument . . . only once or twice in 53 year. In the funeral parlor, when they closed the coffin, I said to her, "Aufwiedersehen." See you again. . . .

Next month I'm going to my older daughter near Seattle. They bought a place up there about a year ago, and they want to change the garage. It's an older house, and the second bedroom is kinda patched on. They gonna change the structure so they can go in through a hall on the west side. I can do carpenter work. I did lots of it on the house on the farm. And if my daughter lets me, I can do the supervising. But I want to hire at least two or three guys to do the tearing down and nailing.

(My first impression was that all the ingredients for a lonely, fading life were present in William Eckhardt's daily life. His legs pained him; no one but his children visited him and his social involvement is limited to his lunches at the Senior Center. He doesn't read, and his principal activities are jigsaw puzzles and needlepoint.

What keeps the guy going, I asked myself? The answers, I think, lie in his determination. His legs hurt, but he walks to the Senior Center. Since friends don't visit him, he goes to play cards with them at the Center. He doesn't read, so he compensates with jigsaw puzzles and needlepoint. And rather than sitting back and reminiscing about the carpentry he has done, he is planning and looking forward to reconstructing his daughter's garage.

I sensed also that he takes a great deal of pride in his accomplishments . . . on the farm, in his marriage and family, and in his handiwork. More than anything else, though I saw him as a man at peace with himself. That's a pretty sustaining combination.)

2
My Cup Runneth Over

(My next door neighbor told me I'd have to meet her "incredible" grandmother, Millie Osgood, who at age 89, was recuperating from cataract surgery but still working as the bookkeeper in her son's business.)

During World War II, I went to work and I've been working ever since. It was quite an experience for me. I had never worked in my life. But I made some very good friends at work, and I've always been glad that I did. Momma never worked. In that generation, not many women did. I wasn't educated for anything. I started to work while we were in Washington, D.C. That was quite an experience too. My husband had a tire retreading business there and he appeared before the Senate to explain the tires they were using for aviation. I really started working back there.

My daughter said, Momma, why in the world don't you take a Civil Service examination?" And I said, "Sis, it's years and years since I've been to school. I'm scared to." So I just took the first job that was available. There were plenty of them, so I went to work in one of the big department stores. We didn't stay in Washington long. The climate was unbearable and my husband's business kind of fell off. So we came back out here. He went to work for the shipyards until his health fell off, and I had to go to work again. I worked in a department store here in town for 22 years as a salesperson. That's about it. And here I am. I've been retired from there for quite awhile, you know.

But after I was out of the department store, why, my son needed someone to come in to do his bookkeeping. He reminded me that my father was good at numbers, and he said to me, "Momma, you're good at numbers too." And I said, "I don't know what you mean . . . good at numbers, but I can use an adding machine." My grandaughter had been doing the books, but she was going to Europe and she wanted to turn them over to me. So I went down there, and I really suffered at first. I didn't know how to do any bookkeeping or anything. I sort of taught myself, but I didn't think I could ever do it. But now I've been doing it a good many years. I make out the State tax, and I keep the books and the bank account and that sort of thing. But I don't make out the Federal tax. I tried it one month and I really messed it up. So I said, "Nope, the accountant has gotta do that." But usually it's not too much. It's not a tremendous job. It's a small business, but it gets hectic sometimes, you know.

Sometimes I think I'd like to quit, but then I think . . . no. It's this thing of being home here, handicapped and not being able to drive yet. They won't let me drive because I can only use one eye. I think I could drive, but it makes me too nervous. Anyway, I'm dependent on someone to drive me down to the business. Usually my son comes up and gets me and brings me home. He also takes care of my eye . . . changes the dressing. There's nothing like having wonderful children.

I usually go down to work about noon. I have lunch here at home, because there's no place to eat down there. If you don't bring your lunch, you're stuck. Last Saturday this fellow that works there had to go to San Francisco and he wanted to get an early start, so it meant that I came down early. And I answered the phone and I saw some people . . . whoever comes in . . . that sort of thing. So I'm just the office girl, and the bookkeeper and the whole thing. Somebody'll call up and say they'd like to talk to the bookkeeper, and I say, "You are." So it keeps me pretty busy, you know. Sometimes when I get home, if I've had a lot of extra things to do down there, I've had it. I'm tired.

I think the thing that keeps me going is that I'm active. I

keep going. I don't stop. I just don't stop. I think people that just stop and sit down . . . it's pretty hard on them. But, of course, I've aches and pains. Don't think that I don't. But I get by with them. I go to my son's business every day. That keeps me going. Before I go down there, I do my housework and things like that.

Another thing that keeps me going is that I'm a student of Unity. It's a philosophy mostly taught in church. And I have studied quite a bit for 10 or 12 years. I think it helps a lot. I think that Unity has helped me more than anything in the last few years. Their philosophy is that there is one God and one Presence. Everything goes around that. They have many wonderful books. You could read them and get more out of them than I could possibly tell you. They do accomplish a great deal. If you are in deep trouble, why you can just have prayers. And sometimes they work and sometimes they don't. It depends on you . . . whether you're receptive enough to them. The family . . . we're a closely woven family and we have lots of get-togethers . . . they got so they never asked me to do anything on Sunday, because they knew I was going to church. But I told them now, not to regard that so much anymore. I wasn't quite that strict.

But I've even worked out a way to get to a church in Hayward. It's way out on 18th Street, and I wasn't much for driving and finding a parking place and all that. So I found out accidentally one day that I could drive down . . . before this operation on my eye . . . and park by the BART station and get a 45 bus, and it went right within a few steps of the church . . . no transfers or anything. When someone told me I could do that, with no transfers, I decided there's nothing keeping me from doing it. So I went there fairly regularly. Of course, with this cataract condition I haven't been going any place too much besides to work.

I do want to keep driving the car. I have a tough time with them out there at Motor Vehicles. They make you take a driver's test, and they give you a license for one year. Of course, I was having this eye problem, and I couldn't see those little bitty numbers, and I always get mad when I think about it, because who ever has to see those tiny numbers when you're driving a car? You don't! You have to see the big signs and, of course, you see traffic, but they put you through the test anyway. When I take a driver's test, I persevere. Of course, I passed the written test all right. Then they made me drive and there was one thing that I did that I never could correct, but that was only one point. That's happened to me every year. You can do the stupidest things when you're taking those tests. The last two times, there was this big man that gave the test to me and I said to him, "Now look, I've got to have this license!" And I made it, and I was so delighted. I said to myself, "My cup runneth over," because I was so pleased.

My eyes may be better after this operation. At night, the lights used to blind me, so I just made a rule I wouldn't drive after dark. People thought I was afraid. I'm not. I've been coming here in the house years and years . . . 40 years . . . by myself, in the middle of the night sometimes, and never think anything about it. But the lights blinded me so that it made me nervous, so I don't drive at night anymore. So I just said that if I have to go out at night, someone will have to come up and get me and bring me back. So that's the way we do. I go down for family gatherings or whatever comes along. We've all had Thanksgiving and Christmas in this house for years. My children have the feeling of wanting to come here.

I have a very small pension and I live on Social Security. That's it. But I get along very well. It's enough for me to live independently. Of course, my pension from the department store is very low. It's only $22. When I worked there, they were forced to have some kind of pension, but they had nothing else . . . no sick leave . . . nothing at all. But finally they worked it out. They gave you a dollar a month for every year that you worked there. Since then they've had to raise it, but that's what it was then. But it comes in pretty handy, that extra money.

And I don't collect a cent from my son. I did when I first started there, but I don't anymore. What would I do with the money if I had it? I go because I'm helping him out. I don't have a lot of money, but I have enough to get along on. I eat right and do as I please, and keep up the car insurance and kinds of things like that that are extras. And, of course, living alone you don't have as many expenses. Of course, the utility bill is what gets you now. I'm very glad I went to work when I did. Social Security has been a blessing to me, it really has.

Sometimes I wonder . . . Well, how much longer? I have one dear friend . . . she's about 93 now, and she's active and around her house every day but she doesn't get out. She has a heart condition and she's well aware of it. I don't know . . . I try not to dwell on things like that. I don't think it's good. I know I've slowed down in a lot of ways. And I do forget, I know, but I haven't a very good memory anyway. The other day I thought maybe I've changed more than I realize. . . . You know, when you have something to do, you just don't stay in bed and get up and think, well, what'll I do? When you've got something to do that you want to do . . . something to look forward to . . . but I don't know whether I'm kidding myself or not. I try not to think about death. A lot of times I think . . . well, this'll be an experience . . . another experience. It's like stepping from one door into another.

I think I would have liked, when I got out of high school . . . Momma and Poppa could have sent me to the University of Texas, but instead they said, "Oh, put it off a year. You're so young," and all that sort of thing. But then I got married and that was the end of that. But I think I would go back. I would like to go to school more. I don't think there's anything can take the place of it. And when I had my children, I made up my mind that I was going to see to it that they got a university education. I always felt that my husband did things that he didn't want to do to make a living. He'd have been a much happier person if he had something he could really enjoy doing. And I wanted it to be so for my children. So I did. I got them both through university. I always thought that if I had my life to live over, I would have done that. What I would have done afterwards, or what I would have studied, I don't know. Maybe philosophy.

(*Driving away from Millie's house, I wasn't sure what I had captured on the tapes. But later on that evening, while I was checking over the recorder and getting the tapes ready for an interview I was to have the next evening, I played back the end of Millie's conversation, which had been cut short by a phone call from her daughter, Sis. I heard the phone ring on the tape, and I heard the enthusiasm in Millie's voice as she answered "Hello-o-o-o . . . Hi!" And I knew why my neighbor had called her "incredible." There is no other way to say it except that everything Millie does is pervaded by her enthusiasm. She has the vitality I would have expected of a 39 year old or a 59 years old; I was astounded to find it an 89 year old lady.)*

3

I Learn by Going
Where I Have to Go

(All I knew about Bud Hobart *before I met him
were the few words a friend had written on the
note that listed his address and phone number.
. . . "Retired teamster and long-time peace
worker. Into disarmament. Went on cross U.S.
walk." I met him in the lobby of his church.*
Bud *is 70.)*

I have a teamster pension and Social Security . . . that's all.
That provides enough. You probably realize that if you draw
your Social Security at 62, you get a less amount than if you
draw it at 65, but I figured it takes 10 years to make up for that,
and I thought . . . I'm going to live for more than 10 years, so
I'm going to lose by it, but I decided I needed the money now,
so what the hell, I'm going to live it up. So I draw Social
Security, which amounts now to about $293 a month, and the
teamster pension, which has been increased to about $400.
The woman that I live with here in San Francisco now generally tries to avoid putting me to any expense. She doesn't earn
any money, but she's usually dieting, so we live frugally. We
run into the same problem that everybody else does . . . rent. I
don't drive a car anymore for several reasons. One is to avoid
the expense and another is to avoid the additional pollution. I
think people should do that if they're able. And I get to ride
the Muni for 5¢.

I was quite active in this church. I was Chairman of the

Social Concerns Committee, and I was very active in the peace movement, and I went to jail a few times opposing the Viet Nam war. And so, when I retired, I thought . . . now I'll be able to devote my full time to all these causes that I could devote only fragments to before. . . . I had some friends down in Davenport, and I was welcome there, so I spent a lot of time down there. But I found myself in a situation I had not faced. I found myself not doing anything for all those causes. First of all I was practically living in Davenport, and it was beautiful and I loved it and I didn't want to give that up to come back to San Francisco to devote myself in fragments to all the causes that I used to find worth spending time on. I found that when I had full time to devote, it was a totally different problem. I had to see some one thing that was worthwhile spending full time on. I wasn't willing to do those fragments anymore.

At first I just started walking around Davenport. I enjoyed each day. Oh, each one was just great! A lot of the time I lived there by myself. My friends stayed over at the place where they worked and just came to their place in Davenport on weekends. So I took care of the place and just loved it. I loved being alone in it. And I walked around and looked at the wildflowers, and I tried to learn their names. And that was one year.

The next year I put in an extensive garden. I worked very hard and enjoyed it. And each day seemed perfect. I had to choose between very delightful ways of spending my time . . . swimming in the creek, walking, gardening, cutting wood for the winter. I just loved it! Each day was great! It didn't bother me much, but I had a little feeling that these great days didn't in total add up to anything.

And then I made a trip back East to visit my sister, and when I came back to San Francisco, I heard about the Walk. And I immediately decided to go on it. I guess that decision really goes back to my high school days. I was influenced greatly by a very puritanical teacher, who, in his conclusions, disagreed with everything I have ever believed in the years since then. But I learned from him . . . he valued justice and accuracy and things like that that really impressed me.

I went to Stanford in 1928, a supporter of Herbert Hoover, and I made friends with students in the college YMCA, which, in those days, was a far out, disregarded organization. Two of my friends were Socialists and debaters for the Socialists in college debates. Four years later, in 1932, I was the Socialist representative in a similar debate. I joined the Socialist Party in 1932, and then I began to study Marxism and became a Marxist. So, as I said, the decision to go on the Walk goes back quite a few years.

Anyway, five years ago yesterday, which was my 70th birthday, I was on the Walk across the United States, and I was walking out of Albuquerque on that day. It was a Continental Walk for Disarmament and Social Justice. It started officially in San Francisco, and we walked to Washington, D.C., arriving there in the middle of October. I was by far the oldest person on the Walk, and I was also the most stubborn and cantankerous. I had my own views, and they did not agree with the views of many others. I had lots of conflicts. I conflicted with the leadership for several reasons . . . one, because I believed a walk was a walk, and I intended to walk all the way, which I did. I walked all but eight miles of the way to Washington. Also, I really believed in disarmament . . . unilateral disarmament . . . I still do. I happen to think that ideas are important. I think it's important to think they're important enough to try to do something about them, and not be dissuaded by others . . . and important enough for you to put yourself out about. . . . Anyway, that was the best year of my life.

But I found even then that while I could enthuse people when I was speaking about disarmament, nobody really shared those beliefs. So I'm a little lonely and discouraged now, and I'm sure the world is going to be blown to hell in the reasonably short future . . . maybe not in my lifetime, very possibly in yours, but very certainly in the lifetime of my grandson, who is very important to me.

One thing I have . . . whether this is good or bad, I don't know . . . but I think I have made my peace with death. I don't want to die, although not having the relationship that I want

with the woman I'm living with makes me think sometimes
... well, what the hell! It's partly that I'm not as satisfied with
my life as I used to be, for two reasons. One, I was satisfied
because I was really working for a cause then. And secondly,
I'm kinda dissatisfied now because I'm pulled in two ways
. . . between my relationship in San Francisco with this
woman, and my life in Davenport. The thing that really holds
me now is my grandson, but I think he'll be going away, and I
don't know what I'll do then. Maybe I'll just stay in Davenport. I was really happy down there. I wrote poems for myself.
I read them once in a while to friends, and that I enjoy more
than anything but I haven't written anything in a long, long
time. I think the greatest thing would be to make music and
write poetry.

One of the great problems with life, I think ... it's terribly
important to be an individual ... to be alone. I like to be alone.
I loved it in Davenport when I was alone. On the other hand,
it's very important to be part of a community. There are many
levels of community, and, for me, a basic one is one-to-one
with a mate. But I don't have it in a satisfactory fashion. I also
want to be a part of a larger community. . . .

I'm 70 and I can't escape it. What I have found is that, in
general, I get along with young people . . . men and women
. . . better than with people my own age. I don't know why
that's so, but I do like young people. . . .

You know, I'm torn in two totally different ways when I
think about what's good about life or how to live. One is the
desirability of being really caught up in this disarmament
thing. I'd really like to try to do something about that. On the
other hand I'd like to just be out in the country and walk and
try to write poems. But . . . you know, there's a couple of lines
of poetry by Theodore Roethke that I claim for my own: "I
wake but take my waking slow / I learn by going where I have
to go."

*(Bud was the first person I interviewed. Except for those two
powerful lines of poetry he quoted at the end . . . lines which I
have quoted myself many times since . . . I felt discouraged by*

*the interview. What kind of introduction to old age was this?
... a man with a commitment to peace strong enough to make
him walk across the United States but who believed that the
whole world was going to blow up? ... a man who longed for
intimacy but who liked being alone?*

*As I got some distance from the interview, however, I saw
something in Bud that I hadn't paid much attention to before.
True, he was a man in conflict, uncertain of where he wanted
to go and with whom he wanted to travel. But I asked myself
how many people his age are struggling to find out what they
want for themselves. Not many. Not many. But Bud has far
too much energy and far too much turmoil churning around
to sit back for very long and contemplate what might have
been. He has to go somewhere, and he will learn by going. I'm
glad I interviewed him.)*

4

I Will Lift Up My Eyes Unto the Hills

(The featured speaker and guest of honor at a luncheon I attended was Elaine Wirth. *She was being honored at her retirement at age 85 from the job she had held at a Senior Center for the previous 20 years. Coincidentally, I caught her on a television program a week later. She was a "must" on my list of people to be interviewed. I met her at her home in El Cerrito.)*

You're catching me in what I call my "impeachment pants." I put them on to take advantage of what looked like a sunny day to do some necessary work in my garden, and that's why I'm wearing them. They are very precious to me, these old Levi's. They were my sister's, and when I first bought the house, she sent them to me to inspire me to work in the garden. But year after year, they began to get pretty worn in the knees. So I decided to cut the cuffs off and turn them into two beautiful patches. And I sat hour after hour watching the impeachment proceedings and the judiciary sessions on TV while I sewed the patches on, and I've called them my "impeachment pants" ever since. As you can see, I have lots of years ahead in the garden . . . the patches aren't even dented.

You'll have to see my garden, because if you want to get any kind of picture of me, you have to see it. I work hard in it. It's an important activity for me. It was the garden that made me buy the place, even before I saw the inside of the house. The real estate agent took me around the south side of the house around 4:30 or 5:00 one afternoon in 1959, and I said to her, "This is the house I want." And she said, "You haven't even seen the inside yet." I said, "I've seen the trees. This is what I want." And I've never regretted it. I have five redwoods and two pines. The garden has been one of the secrets of my vigorous health, I'm sure. I don't mow the lawn, but I do all the planting and weeding and a lot of the pruning. I have such professional pride in it, because it's what I have to sell the students who come here to live.

You know, I share the house with graduate students. This was my retirement project. My brother helped me to buy the place because I didn't have enough money to buy it. He helped with the renovation, which cost more than the house, and now I have four bedrooms, each with its own bath. I manage the place and I pay no rent. I pay all the utility bills, and at the end of the year my brother reimburses me for them. So I'm just the manager here.

All through the 18 years I've had students living here in my house. It's been a marvelous thing for me . . . the combination of young people in the house and the discipline of not getting too involved in their lives. I have a tendency to get too motherish at times . . . when they're not eating right, you know . . . so I tell myself to "get away. Leave 'em alone." I try to keep men. I've never had women . . . women are such a nuisance . . . wanting to do laundry, laundry, laundry and cooking, cooking, cooking.

One of the first things I show my students is the garden, because there are places in the rear where they can study, do their typing, have parties. It's a charming place for entertaining. The students have had big graduation parties out there. Twenty-five Chinese men and their girls one time, 25 Japanese another . . . lots of festive occasions. One day, the entire Chemistry Department . . . wives, children and all . . . had a big barbecue out back. So the garden is the essential part of the house, not just for me, but for the people who share the property with me.

And it's been particularly gratifying to me because I had a

very small salary while I was working at the Senior Center. And before that, when I left the YWCA in 1958, I was being paid the top salary, and I was so pleased with myself that I had reached the pinnacle of financial independence. I kept putting extra money into my retirement fund . . . I called it my rocking chair fund . . . and thank God I did, because now the only real income I have is my YWCA check which is $152.60 and Social Security which is $280.60.

I've worked for so little all these years, but money hasn't been the goal. I have managed to keep my VW up and I managed to go to the symphony and the opera. The money I've had, I just spent on me. It bought my food, my entertainment, my transportation, with no drain. Think how I've been spared. So many old people have to pay rent. I could never have faced that problem. I've been so lucky in so many ways.

Since I retired from the Senior Center, I'm busier than ever, and I don't know where the time goes. My latest project is helping to organize a new political party called the World Citizens Party: California, along with several of the people from the Friday Forum, which I'll tell you about in a minute. And I'm active in the United World Federalists . . . I have been since it began. I've been a member of the American Civil Liberties Union from the beginning. I've been a member of the Democratic Party and I was precinct chairman in this area for a good many years, but I can't spend the energy climbing the stairs to deliver the literature any more. There are still some people I see on the streets here who say, "There's the Dollars-for-Democrats lady."

Oh, I still walk two or three miles a day. I go to the bank, the grocery store . . . pay my bills . . . all of this I do walking. I force myself to do it even though I still drive my car, but I do it because I know I must, because it's good for my circulation. I've been very lucky in health, really. I have no stomach problems, no digestion problems . . . never had headaches in my life. My eyes are beginning to fail though. I have cataracts coming, but the doctor says, "Oh, I think you'll be dead before they're operable." But they are dimming. I can't see, for instance, when I go to a symphony or a concert which of the singers is performing.

I still read as much as my eyesight will let me. I try to keep up with the current magazines. I take the *New Republic*, the *Saturday Review of Literature, Harpers, Atlantic Monthly* . . . I've taken the *Atlantic* for a thousand years. So if I get through these I do pretty well. I haven't done as much with the theater on account of my hearing. I'm experimenting with a new hearing aid, and I'm happy that I've conquered the frustration that hit me two years ago when I tried one that nearly drove me crazy. I took it back and said, "This is not for me. I'll learn sign language instead." And I started to learn it and made some progress in it, but I'm not faithful in going to classes because I'm too busy. . . .

My mother and father were Illinois people. My father was a young lawyer and my mother was a teacher. They already had two other children when they moved to Denver just in time to drop me, in the beginning of winter in 1892. There were eventually five of us children in the family, and I think it was almost too much for my mother, because she hadn't wanted another baby. She wanted two boys and two girls, and she got them, and then along came the fifth one. . . . My mother died young. She was 56 . . . very young. Anyway, I was so excited about the new baby. I used to swing on the front gate and say to the children, "Do you want to see our new baby brother?" It's a wonder I didn't charge to let them in. My mother said I could give him his bath, and she showed me how, and I really took care of him as a tiny baby, so I've always called him my baby brother. He's 76 now and we're very proud of one another.

We grew up in a very happy home, with ideals for excellence in education. My father was quite a Latin scholar and my mother did a number of things with art and painting. We had no music background and no language background, and this I regret, because I was never urged, except for Latin, to learn or familiarize myself with French or Spanish.

My father became a very prominent, but not wealthy lawyer, very much interested in the need of the common people for legal advice. When he died, it was the common people . . . hundreds of them . . . that came to his funeral. He died when he was 49 and I was 16. He had a stroke on Lincoln's Birthday and he was never able to go back to his office again. My mother was left with five children, all in the process of being educated. I can still hear my older brother talking to my mother right after the funeral, while I was in bed in the next room. "Don't worry about Elaine. She doesn't have to go to college. We'll just put her in business school. She'll get a job and then she'll get married anyway." And that night I made up my mind that I would go through college.

I had a series of illnesses in my upper teen years, probably over the loss of my father. I was very disturbed about it. But then one of my brother's old sweethearts who was living near San Diego came to visit us, and she saw how run down I was. She asked my mother if she could take me back with her to regain my health. And that's what happened.

After a year, I went back to Denver, did some college work there, and then went to Chicago to the Western College of Expression, because this had become my chief interest. I had imagined myself becoming another Sarah Bernhardt. I remember needing some money at that time, so I went down to visit my grandmother in Decatur at Christmas. When I finally got around to asking her to lend me some money, she popped out of the covers with her cap on . . . we were both sharing a big feather bed, you see . . . and said, "I won't loan you one cent. You should be home in Denver with your mother. I do not approve of your being there in Chicago and living in that house with all those other girls."

My uncle Harry, who was a Congressman, loaned me the money though. He said to me, "Elaine, I want to make a good business woman out of you. I could give you the money, but I'm not going to. You sign a note for it and pay me 2% interest for it," which I did.

I finished up at Western, and it gave me enough training and prestige to get back to Colorado to give dramatic readings, which were very popular in those days. From that time on I made my own living. I worked hard and I got further along in college, and then Sue, the friend from near San Diego, wrote and said she could get me a job, even though I still hadn't quite gotten my B.A., teaching expression and story telling in Anaheim Junior High School, not so very far from Los Angeles. So I went out there in 1915 and it was a great experience for me. It was a great feeling when I got my first paycheck, because I was making almost as much as my older brother, and he had finished law school. . . . That's a flash of triumph I hadn't remembered for a thousand years.

Towards the end of the year, I was rehearsing a play and some people that I didn't know came in to the rehearsal. It turned out they were from Pasadena, and they offered me a job teaching dramatics in the high school after just one year at Anaheim. While I was there I joined the Playhouse, and I acted and directed and produced plays there, which was a very gratifying experience.

After five years, I felt I could teach Broadway a thing or two, so I took my savings and went off to New York, determined to see if I could crash the commercial theater in any capacity, because I was a good actress, I was very able as a stage manager, I knew something about lighting, and I was a good publicity person. I had confidence plus. So it was a terrible blow to me to find indifference in theater people in New York. I had lots of good interviews and nobody turned me away, and I didn't stand outside of doors, but everyone wanted more than I was willing to offer. I was offered the leading lady in a road show performance of a very good play. I had read the lines well, and the director liked my work very much. But just as I was leaving, he said to me, "Oh, one thing more . . . will you sleep with the stage manager?"

Well, my money was dwindling, but I decided to make it stretch until Eleanora Duse came to New York that fall. I bought seats for every play she did, saving just enough money to get back to Pasadena. It's hard for me to talk about that experience, because it was a great emotional peak in my life, in terms of commitment. On the first night I sat in the top row of the balcony, and Duse looked one inch tall. For the last play, I blew myself to the best seat in the house. And it was a terrible rainy afternoon, but I wanted to see this wonderful woman even closer. So after the play was over I decided to be a stage-door-Johnnie and wait till she came out. So I waited under my umbrella, and she finally came out in her car and she saw me and I waved at her. And as the car drove away, she got up on her knees in the back of the limousine and kept waving at me . . . this darling little old lady. She looked very old and tired. And she was. She died within three or four weeks . . . and, you can see . . . I still can't talk about it . . . never have been able to . . . without getting weepy. . . .

I didn't marry until I was 36. I met my husband while I was teaching in Anaheim. I was good friends with his sister and I used to visit her house a lot. He was coming in and out of town all the time . . . he was an oil engineer and travelled a lot. He was married at the time, but he finally got a divorce and then . . . well, I had known him six or seven years . . . we were married.

I never got pregnant. I thought about it a number of times and couldn't quite decide, but he had four children already and he was against the idea of starting a new family. . . . I spent most of my married life driving back and forth with him between Fort Worth, Kansas City, and Minneapolis, playing the little theaters whenever we were there long enough. I also found time to get my Master's degree in dramatic arts during that period.

You know, it was in the theater that I began to think more about others . . . about internationalism. It was a production of Galsworthy's *Strife*. I'll never forget that night . . . it hit me like a blow between the eyes with somebody's fist. We were working on that dreadful scene with the Coal Strike in England, and there's this bitter scene between Roberts, the leader of the strikers and his wife who was suffering so. She was ill and there was no food or heat or coal in the house and she's asking him which is more important . . . life for his family or sticking out for a principle. And I said to myself, "What am I wasting my time for . . . showing theatrical presentations of this kind of thing when it's actually going on all over the world. I better get into it."

And then right about that time, when the Depression was going full blast, my husband died very suddenly. I was terribly shot, but then my old friend, Sue, came to the rescue again. She was head of the YWCA in the Philippines and she called and said "Come on over." So I went to see her in Manila, thinking I'd stay for a month or two, but I stayed over a year, doing volunteer work.

I campaigned for women's suffrage with these two marvelous women who spoke the local dialects wherever we went. And whenever we got to some little village, the residents would always ask me to talk a little in English so the children could hear it. I would rattle off anything I could think of, but I got some platform experience.

A little later when we were supposed to visit a leper colony on the island of Culion, these two women, who were both very frightened of leprosy, asked me if I would do the talk, using a translator. They told me "There are 800 votes down there, and they might be enough to swing the whole election." I have a photograph of myself, dressed up in a mestiza dress, speaking English to 800 leper women. They just sat like blank logs while I was speaking, but when the translator would tell them what I said, they really came to life. It was one of the most fascinating experiences I've ever had. And when the votes were counted, all 800 women had voted in favor of women's suffrage!

At the end of my year there, I was sent as a delegate to the International Conference of Education Associations in Tokyo. That was right at the beginning of the Japanese War, and things were very tense at the conference. But anyway, I met someone who was very influential in school broadcasting in Great Britain, and we became very interested in one another. She knew I was at loose ends and she offered to help me get a fellowship to get some training in that kind of work. Well, it's a long story, but I got the fellowship, and in April of the next year, I went over to London. So it all worked together.

This is the fascinating thing about my life. Each episode has led happily into the next. It's been rewarding and profitable intellectually, and it's kept me eating. I've never had lots of money, but I've been comfortable and never in real want of anything. . . .

I finished the fellowship and then I came to New York where I put in a year and a half writing radio scripts for the Columbia Graduate School of Education. But then the War came along and they scrapped the whole idea of school broadcasting.

So, again, here I am. What do I do now? Well, I had been closely linked with the YWCA after having worked with Sue, so I went to work for the USO division of YWCA, and I worked all over the world for them for the next 18 years . . . until I retired in 1959. . . a patchy life. . . .

I have friends from way, way back. In all my USO jobs, moving around all over the world, I had to build support for the programs. I had to build a Board of Directors and collect girls for junior hostesses for the servicemen, so that I had close and intimate contact with, maybe, three or four hundred girls in each community. And it has always been a real joy to me at Christmas time to hear from almost all those places . . . Naples, Italy . . . Richmond, Virginia . . . Seattle, Washington . . . the Philippines . . . the same thing all over the world. So I have these long ties reaching into my past that are renewed briefly, and some of them even remember my birthday.

This one friend, Sue, who brought me to my first job in Anaheim, is very ill in a nursing home in Rhode Island. I saw her two years ago, and she's becoming disoriented and going down. . . . As I look through my old Christmas card list now, I'm beginning to check off . . . dead . . . dead . . . dead. But I never say "How sad." I say, "Good! She got out of it while she was still active, while she was still doing things." And that's all I ever want anybody to say about me. To say it's sad that all my friends are dying is not a sensible thing. The best approach is to feel you can finish up while you're still capable of doing things. The sad thing is to end up like Sue, who has so many capabilities and who has done so much to help alleviate suffering throughout the world, and who now is suffering herself, and so deformed arthritically.

And this is the challenge I like to throw to scientists. I

think the time has to come when people like Sue will be allowed to ask to get out, and have their requests granted, realizing that there is no means of support and that there aren't enough people to care. The financial strain on our hospital and medical services is too great. I feel very strongly about this afterlife nonsense. When we're ready to be scrapped, I say, "Let's get it over with." I believe in the recycling process. We all go back into the process, as all of life and all living things do . . . in an evolutionary sense.

I feel that way every time I drive over to San Francisco and I see the tides that go in and out of the Bay. And it's strange how I finally came to get this feeling about water. If I had stayed in Colorado, I don't know what would have happened, but I did lean a great deal on the strength of the mountains there. I used to quote the line, "I will lift up my eyes unto the hills," because of the reassurance I got. And I get this same reassurance from the waters of the Bay. It probably comes only where we can see the cycle of renewal every few hours from the tides. . . .

Religion . . . church-going religion . . . has meant absolutely nothing to me. I joined the West End Church in New York just to please my boss, because I was going to a Catholic country to work, but it was just for the form. She also asked if I had a black dress. I said I hadn't, and she said, "Elaine, you just can't go to Naples without some black clothes." So I went to Saks in New York and bought two black dresses, which I still have. But religious fervor is so foreign to me. I couldn't possibly participate in the Indian religion, for example, that the young people seem to be so interested in . . . the chanting and so forth. I don't need that.

I have gone to the Unitarian Church on occasion, but I don't go regularly. I contribute to it when I find some extra money rolling up hill, but that's the only church to which I do contribute. I admire the Unitarians tremendously because of their desire to bring all people together regardless of their race or their faith. And it doesn't have the emotionalism that seems to sway other religious groups.

Some of the satisfactions that other people get from reli-

gion, I get from world affairs, trying to become an internationalist. This, I'm sure, goes back to my early beginnings
. . . to my father and to my uncles, both of whom were in Congress. It was through them that I came more in touch with the wideness of the world. One of the joys of working in this community has been the proximity of so many different groups of people. I rejoiced in being thrown right into the different communities right after I got here. I organized groups of Chinese old people and Blacks from West Oakland right in the same Center. And the same thing with the Filipinos and Japanese and Caucasians. It was a marvelous mixture of people, and to see them coming together gave me a thrill. I think that the energy I have comes from the satisfaction of seeing some of this come together and meld.

I experienced that thrill just last Friday, when we took the first steps in another enterprise . . . organizing the old people in the federally sponsored housing projects into something called Seniors for Quality Education. This has come into being as the result of a long confrontation with the bureaucracy, which, philosophically, I'm sure, looks on old people as discards. They're willing to provide high school and grammar school playpen sort of things. But what do they do in those buildings to keep those people mentally alive? They simply will not spend the money to hire university level people to satisfy these people . . . to get them to come down to the meeting rooms and make them know there's a world out there that is worth looking at, and that it's exciting and rewarding.

On Friday we had 10 or 11 young social workers who service the buildings come to our Friday Forum at the Senior Center to see us demonstrate to them how possible it is to get old people intently listening . . . to hear someone talk about what's happening in the Middle East or on the Horn of Africa and how it relates to them. What is the connection between what's going on there and here? These social workers were just wide-eyed! And to hear them talk about those old people
. . . why, most of them are just in their thirties and forties themselves. They think of them as I think of my friend, Sue, in

that nursing home, just patiently waiting to die. They've had a great deal of trouble getting the old people down to meetings, to talk about their gripes and what they want changed in their houses. That's understandable. These people have long since given up on having anything changed, because in the bureaucracy nothing ever changes.

The Friday Forums are the reason I came to California. I had retired from my job with the USO in April, 1959, and I got a phone call from this woman I had known in the YWCA, and she asked me, "Will you come out here to help with these old people?" So I got in my Volkswagen and drove across the country and went right to work . . . for the next 19 years, as a matter of fact. At that point, there were 12 very old people sitting around a ping-pong table, meeting every Friday, each bringing a news clipping which they would read aloud. And there were no comments, nobody did any research, nobody did any reading. We began to talk about changing things. Was everybody registered? No, nobody was registered. So we got them registered and we started bringing in candidates as elections came near, we got college professors to talk to them, and ever since then it just widened and widened. We have 100 to 125 people at each Forum, and I've never had to recruit, never had to advertise. It's just word of mouth. Even when the bus strike was on we had 70 or 75 people that would walk two or three miles, which was good for them. They got there. They wouldn't miss 'em.

This is the thing . . . to have confidence that it's possible to have changes in older people's lives. I say it's wonderful to be old! If we can just spread the feeling that it's the best time of our lives. Grab it! Get it! . . . each day that you can. Never a boring time! . . . The only difference for me now is that there's less time to look ahead . . . less time to show my commitment. And I have commitment! A lot of people are not committed to anything, and this is sad. . . .

You know, I'm concerned about the amount of time that people spend in nostalgia, and here you've tempted me to be too nostalgic. It's fun to do it now and then, but to get into a pattern of living in the past, as so many people do, in my experience at the Center . . . continually talking about "the good old days when I could do this or that" . . . this I think is one of the stultifying things . . . one of the corroding influences on older people. I would use, and do use, everything in my power to keep people looking forward and feeling that here's their last chance to do something . . , and to keep them planning for the days ahead . . . and to keep asking themselves, "What is it that I haven't been able to do . . . that I want to do . . . that I must do?"

(Elaine's energy and her zest for life are as beautiful to observe as her words are to read. Each time I have met her, I have departed feeling more wholesome and more reassured about my later years. One Sunday afternoon, I returned to give her a copy of the manuscript of our interview. While she was reading it, I was reading a copy of a term paper she had written for a Social Welfare class at the University of California when she was 67. The last lines are about Haley's Comet:

"I was 18. I think now that the Comet must have done something to me permanently: I hadn't taken too long a look down the years, then. Knowing that it had been in our sky in 1759, in 1835, and now in 1910, knowing that it would come again in 1985—just like clockwork—gave me a feeling of safety in such an ordered Universe. The long, long cycle of life seemed secure and purposeful. Oh, if I could just see that Comet once again now that I know more about living!"

Her eyes are just beginning to fail, but she has greater vision than any person I've known.)

5

I've Had My Life . . .
I Have No Fear of Death

(Sheldon Greenwald *is the stepfather of a*
friend. He is 85 and just now closing up his
practice of law. He lives in a handsome one
bedroom apartment near the top of Nob Hill in
San Francisco.)

When I first went to school, one of my idols was Abraham
Lincoln. He was a lawyer. I used to say, "When I grow up, I
want to be like Lincoln." The idea of being a lawyer stuck
with me all the time. From the time I was six or seven years
old, I never varied from that idea . . . that I wanted to be a
lawyer.

I went to Yale Law School for a year and got my J.D. at
Boalt Hall in Berkeley. But I think I went through law school
too early. I was only 18 when I graduated from the University
of California. I wasn't 21 when I had finished my law course. I
think I would have taken more time and I think I would have
a better record if I'd gone to school at a more normal age. I saw
myself falling behind when all my classmates were going
ahead, and I couldn't do anything about it because I was
going through so many difficulties with my family. I'm sure I
would have accomplished a great deal more in the field of law.

But I've been practicing law for 64 years, and I'm just
now winding down my affairs. I had a heart attack a year ago
May, and when I got out of it, I decided it was time for me to
quit practicing. I still have a few little matters . . . a few trusts

and wills and probates that I've been handling which don't take up too much of my time, but I'm not taking any new business at all.

I usually walk down to the office around 9:30 in the morning. I don't walk back on account of the hills. I usually come back here around two o'clock and lie down on my bed and take a nap for an hour or so. The newspaper comes about four o'clock. Then I go out for dinner two or three times a week, but if I stay home, I fix a salad and a bowl of soup for myself. I don't eat a great deal. The doctor took 20 pounds off me when I was at the hospital, and he doesn't want me to gain any more. And I don't have the appetite I used to. . . .

I do quite a bit of reading. You can see some of the stuff I've got strewn around all over the place. I like current literature and I enjoy history very much. I've bought all the Will Durant books and I've read most of them. Then there's *Harry S. Truman* by Margaret Truman, and *Burr* by Gore Vidal . . . and *Eleanor and Franklin*. I've always been a history buff. I started when I was seven years old. One of the first books I ever got in my life was a child's story of *The Iliad* and *The Odyssey*.

I was born in 1893 in San Francisco. I was about four years old when my mother and father were divorced, and I was raised by my mother and my grandparents. My mother never remarried, and I lived with her until I was 58 years old. She was very possessive and I had a lot of difficulties as I grew up and reached manhood. She was 80 when she died. I found myself all alone and I was really desperate. I could very easily have committed suicide. I was free, but I was sort of helpless.

You remember the picture *Of Human Bondage* with . . . what's their names? . . . Leslie Howard and Bette Davis. Well, I saw that picture and that was the first time I realized that *I* was in human bondage. So, after the experience of watching that picture, I decided that I was going to make a break for it. I was going to do something. That's when I consulted a psychiatrist. I went to him and told him what was happening to me and my mother, and I said I thought she needed some psychiatric help. He said, "You need it," so I started going.

But I couldn't get away from my family for ten minutes. Everywhere I went the whole family went along with me . . . my mother, my grandmother, and my grandfather. When I went to Yale, they packed up and moved to New Haven with me. I went to Los Angeles for an extended trial down there, and they moved down there with me. I just didn't know what I was going to do.

Around World War II . . . I couldn't get into World War I because I was underweight . . . I was so desperate to escape that I went down to the Navy to enlist. I said to myself, "To hell with it! If I make it, my mother will have to work it out for herself." The Navy examined me and I was fit enough, but there were no openings for someone at my age with my skills. So I never got into World War II either.

My mother was very difficult about my getting out at nights, and when I decided to accept leadership in the Masons, in which I had been somewhat active, we had quite a few fights about that. But I stuck to it and three years later I became Master of my Lodge. There was another Lodge called the Research Lodge, and I was Master of that for awhile. As the name implies, there's a lot of hisory about Masonry that you don't get just going through the degrees and sitting through meetings. I wrote a number of treatises on the history and things like that. Those were the things I felt that I could do . . . to do something extra. I would have liked to have gone into some public service work, but I never had the opportunity. And then, a little later, around the time my mother died, I became President of the Masters and Wardens Association. Still and all, I was getting on in years and I didn't see any future in front of me. I didn't know what I was going to do. But for me, life began when I was 58. I'm 85 now and I'm happier than when I was 40.

I married my wife about six months after my mother died. I had gone to school with Alice . . . that was my wife's name . . . way back in grammar school . . . and I knew her brother and sister-in-law when I went to the University of California. And I met her again five years after I graduated. She had married and was widowed, and after that she married again and was widowed a second time. Her second husband died a little before my mother died. And I started calling on her and started going out together. Six months later I asked her to marry me and she did. Everything that I regard in the way of happiness I've gotten since that time.

We were married about seven or eight years, and, as I said, life began when I was 58. I was treated just as if I were her children's natural father, and, in fact, I legally adopted them. . . . I was doing Masonic work when we were married. We used to go down to Los Angeles where one of my committees met every winter. We'd take a vacation every winter time. I'd go to my meeting, which lasted a couple of days, and then we'd take off to La Jolla or Palm Springs or Death Valley . . . one of those places. Those were very happy experiences. As a matter of fact, Alice and I did quite a lot of travelling. The first thing we did was to go to the Hawaiian Islands. After that I went to Europe twice with her. I remember the second time so well. I came home one day and said, "It's later than we think. Why don't we take another trip to Europe?" I decided to close up my office and forget about my practice. If I lost a couple of months' income, okay. So I said, "Let's go and have another trip." So we did. We were gone for two months. A month later she dropped dead. I've always been glad we made that trip. . . .

I have lots of friends, but very few of them from when I was with my mother. I couldn't normally invite anyone over for a friendly evening, and if I wanted to go out of the house for an evening, she would raise hell. So, most of my friends I've met through Alice. Probably I'm out two or three times a week visiting them, and, of course, I invite them back. I don't do any entertaining here because I'm limited, but we have fine dinners at the Club. I joined the Lagunilla Golf and Country Club after I got married, and I made a lot of friends out there. But, of course, a lot of them are dying off, you know. I notice now that there's only one other member who's older than I am. And every year, somebody that I've been playing golf with drops by the wayside. It's getting to be a normal matter. You feel the loss for a month or so, and then you get accustomed to it. That's about the way it goes. . . .

I go to Temple on the High Holidays. I'm a member of the Temple and I'm involved in some of the activities. We usually have a group of lecturers every fall and I enjoy going to hear them. I go to the parties and to the picnics, but I'm not active in the religious part of it. I don't exactly call myself an atheist . . . probably I'm an agnostic. I know too much about science to make me feel there's such a thing as a personal God. . . . You see, I took a little chemistry when I was in college because I had to take it, and I had taken physics when I was in high school. I had straight A's and I really enjoyed it. And I'm still very interested in all kinds of scientific things.

I'm still playing golf twice a week . . . 18 holes. That is, I'm just beginning to play 18 holes again. After my heart attack a year ago, I wasn't able to play at all. But then I went back to nine holes and now I'm able to play 18 again. I've hardly had any ill moments in my life. When I was a child, I went through the usual whooping cough and measles, and I had my adenoids removed. About 15 years ago I had a prostatectomy which is usual for that age. And about 10 years ago I had a little trouble with my back. I was leaning over to tie my shoe laces and I couldn't get up again, so they took me to the hospital and put me in traction for eight days. I haven't had any trouble with it since. I don't have any excesses and I've been fairly healthy. I started to smoke when I was 21, but the cigarettes left a smell on my fingers, and every time I put them near my mouth, they'd nauseate me. I just couldn't stand smoke, so I quit and I've never smoked since.

I didn't have much of a sex life while my mother was alive, but, of course, after I married I had a good healthy relationship with my wife . . . I drink . . I've always drunk . . . but not to excess. We always had wine and liquor in my grandparents house, and I don't know of a time when I was denied liquor. But I'm not really a drinker and never have been. Oh, I take a drink when I go out, but . . . I think probably the fact that I've been moderate in everything has something to do with my long life. Of course, the advances in science have something to do with it too.

One of my biggest difficulties now is hearing. I've been to

the doctor a number of time and he says I have nerve deafness.
I've got a couple of hearing aids, but they don't do much good,
and I'm not wearing them much any more. I can hear fairly
well, but once in awhile you have to raise your voice a little,
but otherwise it's not bad.

My eyes are okay. I just applied for a new driver's license
and I had no difficulty in going through the eye examination.
They gave me a renewal for four years. I'll be 89 before I need
another one. But I probably won't need a new one then
because I feel that time is running out on me. But it doesn't
bother me. I know my limitations and I don't feel I have the
same mentality and abilities that I had a number of years ago.

And that's another experience. When I had my heart
attack, I was as calm as I am right now talking to you. I was 83
years old and I didn't have the slightest idea I had anything
wrong with me until I fell flat on the floor. But I knew
instinctively that I was having a heart attack even though I
had none of the symptoms they tell you about when you have
an attack. They tell you that you get pains in your upper chest
and down your arms and that you have nausea. I had nothing
like that. I had just taken my shower and I was making up my
bed, and the sheet that I had just picked up fell out of my
hands, and I found myself lying on the floor. And I couldn't
get up.

The telephone was in the room, so I pulled it down and
dialed my doctor. I said, "I've got a heart attack." He said, "I'll
send the ambulance right away." And then I dialed my daughter and told her the same thing. As I was laying there, I said to
myself, "I'm 83 years old. My time is up. It's reasonable. I've
had my life. So what!" The thought of dying didn't bother me
at all. I still marvel at it. It gives me a lot of comfort to know
that I was right there at the point of dying, and I had no fear of
it. And I have no fear of death now.

*So many years of Sheldon Greenwald's early life were
spent, as he put it, "in human bondage." But life began at 58,
when he married for the first time. He lost his wife after less
than eight years, and he says he's happier at 85 than he was 40.*

The incredible thing about Sheldon is not his happiness today . . . that's understandable. It's his resilience from the misery of the earlier years that is so hard to believe . . . and so heart-warming.

A year has passed between the interview and my writing these notes, but I still cannot imagine a more reassuring set of words about old age and dying than Sheldon's as he experienced his heart attack: "My time is up. It's reasonable. I've had my life.")

6

I Haven't Seen Enough
of this Life Yet

*(Taylor "Pat" Patterson is a fireman who
retired from two consecutive careers. He is 77
and looks fifteen years younger than that. He
and his wife Vivian live in a house in an older
part of Richmond.)*

When I was 30, I began to think of myself as approaching old age. I just figured I was getting old. After I was 35, even older . . . and 40, I thought was ancient. And about 45 I commenced to drift back, not to 20 again, but to 30. After that I completely adjusted to the aging process.

I really don't know why, but I had a feeling of anxiety at 30, and after that it seemed to level off. I guess it was because of a career change. I had a lot of disappointments in the way of . . . I don't know how to express it . . . it was the complete unfairness. It was frustrating, because I had worked hard for what I was supposed to get, and I was deliberately passed over, and I guess it roused a little fighting mood in me. Finally, four years and two promotional examinations later, we got it straightened out, and I got my appointment to Captain. After that I began to settle down, so to speak.

Originally there were ten Negroes in the entire department . . . five on one watch and five on another . . . and when I joined, I became the eleventh. There was no place to put me so they assigned me to the department shops, working just like a mechanic, delivering hoses and stuff like that. But I couldn't study for my exams because I was busy being a social lion, with my nights well taken care of. So after a year, I asked to be assigned to the station house in "Siberia," where I could study when there weren't any fires. "Siberia" was where they sent white firemen when they stepped into trouble. The worst punishment they could give 'em was to send 'em to "Siberia."

I'll tell you this . . . when I got to be Captain, my crews kept on their toes. Fighting fire isn't just a matter of grabbing a hose and squirting it on a fire. There's quite a bit involved. There's a lot of techniques you have to go through to insure that you'll come out alive, or to maybe help someone else get out.

I remember once, during a drill, they made a mistake. And all during the ride back to the station, I'm thinking that I've got to say something about it. The guy who made the mistake knows he made it . . . everyone knows it, and I'm figuring out what to say. By the time we backed the rig into the house, heads got together and one of the guys comes over to me and says, "Captain, is it alright with you if we run the rig back out and go through a few of these things again?" I had intended staging a little drill the next time we were out to the drill tower . . . not to make it too obvious. But there was no need to . . . they carried it off themselves. And the next time we went out there, it was letter perfect. I had good crews.

When I retired, they told me they were going to have a dinner for me. I said, "Oh no. I don't want a dinner. I don't want that." I just wanted to get out quietly. They paid no attention and had the dinner and 125 guys came to it. I felt very good about that, but I got a little emotional when I was called upon to say a few remarks. I just knew I was going to flop, but I didn't. It was quite an experience. Sometimes I wish I had stayed. You see, when I got out, I had four years to go. You were supposed to go out at 65, but I was just 61.

The wife and I wanted to travel, but I never had the time. You can't very well go too far in two weeks vacation, which I was getting at the time. So we looked forward to the time when I had all the time to do the things I wanted.

But I became bored with myself after I had retired, because I had no responsibility at all. I was an ardent hunter and fisherman, but somehow they didn't quite suffice. I went to the race track one day about a year after I retired, and I was offered a job in the track Fire Department. I was told they had all thse firemen, but none of them were really trained, and they were afraid that if they ever had a big fire there, the men would panic. I didn't know anything about their set-up, but I went in there and did the job and had a very pleasant stay . . . very pleasant. And I retired a Captain from there too. After I hit 70, I was supposed to retire, but they called me back for another year. I think I could have stayed there longer, but I didn't. I jumped down when I was almost 72.

For the past five years, I've been going to the track steadily. That's my hobby. I know a lot of people there. It's Old Home Week when the track opens. There are touts all over the place, but there are a few people I have confidence in that I met in the past. And that keeps me going, because I'm not going to do anything that costs *me* money. I don't care how much I like it, if I go pretty far in the red, I'm through with it. So, I've done fairly well over the years. And, having worked at the track, we get a little pension from there, and have passes and free parking . . . it's fun. . . .

I had a lot of frustrations when I was young . . . real deep frustrations. You see, when I was a kid, I was supposed to be an invalid. The doctor told my mother I wouldn't survive to an adult, and he advised her not to send me to school until I was seven. I was larger than most kids in the classroom then, and that bothered me. Several of the older white kids in the school . . . there were only three or four blacks besides myself out of the 700 or so in the whole school. Anyway, they decided to chase me out of the school. Maybe they were just hazing me, but I didn't like it. So then an older friend of mine who was a very good boxer taught me to box, and my attitude sort of changed. I disobeyed the principal's order not to fight in the school yard, and I'd fight anywhere . . . school yard, school room, hallways, anywhere that anybody bothered me. Consequently my mother had to spend as much time at school as I did.

I wasn't a bad kid as far as disrespect goes, because my folks taught me that if I ever talked back to a teacher or swore at one or gave any trouble like that, they would deal with me. That wasn't my line, but I would fight. The principal begged me just to tell him the trouble I was having in the school yard, and I said, "Okay, I'll do that, but when they hit me, I gotta hit 'em back." Well, I finally got so I could control myself, but any time anybody challenged me after school, that was my business.

Then, when I got to be around 11 or 12, I ran into another situation. A neighbor whose back yard abutted ours had four or five sons, and one of them was always in trouble. It seems that he went out one night with a gang he was in and broke into an automobile. The police finally caught up with them, and this neighbor across the back fence . . . he was a prominent attorney and I suppose he was trying to shield his son . . . this neighbor said that I was the leader of the gang, and that I was with them, and I did the stealing. All of this was news to me. I didn't know anything about it, but I was yanked out of my classroom. My teacher, whom I respected, told me on the way down the hall to the principal's office, "Just say you did it, and we'll back you up. We'll protect you." From that day on, I hated that teacher and the principal.

I went into high school and had no trouble at all . . . no trouble whatsoever, but the damage had been done. I didn't trust anybody. It wasn't until after I was 30 that I began to trust anybody. There was that situation with the Fire Department . . . they intimated . . . they didn't tell me directly . . . that I ought to be thankful that I had a job as hoseman. So, that's the root of my frustration. I have none now, but it could have wrecked my life.

I have been to San Quentin as a visitor, and I knew some of the prisoners in there. I said to myself, "There, but for the grace of God, go I." I could have been in deep trouble because of the incidents I've told you about. But I got over the frustrations in later life. I've mellowed. . . .

I guess I was interested in girls from the time I was about 12 years old, but I was afraid of them. I was 15, I think, and I was at a party, and there were a lot of girls there, and I was interested in them, but from a far away point. Finally the girls got tired of me just standing around looking at them, I guess, and one by one they'd come up and they'd talk to me and try to make me feel comfortable. Finally one got me in the middle of the floor to dance. I couldn't dance, so she said, "I'll teach you . . . One-two-three-four, one-two-three-four." So that was my start, but even then, two or three years later, I would still be standing way off. I'd be as interested as I could be, but someone had to build a fire under me, I guess. But after I got older. . . .

I'm exceedingly bashful to this day, and some of it sticks out a little. I think that shyness comes from my father. He was the same way. He had lots of friends and everybody seemed to like him, but he was never loud or put himself on anyone. But anyway, I think I began to seek out girls' company when I was about 18. I was lucky . . . my family was well thought of and they had a host of friends. Every now and then someone would call and say, "My niece is coming in," or "My daughter is in town." So I was very lucky in that respect, and I met a lot of girls. For awhile, at 19, 20, 22, 24, 25, I was girl crazy . . . so much so that I wouldn't even think of marriage. And then I met Vi . . . Vivian. I was 28 years old then, and at the time I was going with four or five other girls fairly steady. But I met her, and we seemed to hit it off pretty well. I didn't think we would, but we did. And we've been married for 49 years . . . no separations . . . a few fights, but no one got hurt.

Vi and I don't have any kids . . . she lost one and never conceived again. But my sister got into the Red Cross during the War and she was stationed in Arizona, so Vi and I raised her three kids. And now we have just about taken over another young lady. She's no relative to us, but her mother's a friend of Vi's and she brought her here when she was three years old just to stay until she could find an apartment. But she stayed four or five years, and now we have another "niece" to add to our gang of nieces. . . .

On an average day, I get up late. I like to get up at eight o'clock, but too often it's nine. I fool around doing little or nothing. I try to make it downtown to some of the stores, running errands . . . business to take care of. And I try to keep one little project going all the time, even if it's nothing but fixing a hinge on a door. I'll say this . . . I'm inclined to sit too much. I do that, until Vi puts a bomb under me and moves me right out.

We manage to travel somewhere every year. We've been to Mexico seven or eight times now. I like Mexico. I like it very much, and I guess that's the reason we haven't done too much travelling in the States. Next year, Vi tells me we're going all the way around South America for 54 days. I don't think we will do it, but she does, so maybe we will. All my travelling now is going to be by ship. It's luxury . . . it's easy. When you get aboard ship, you hang up your clothes in a closet, and you don't disturb them till you wear them. No packing till you get off the ship. And the food is excellent and I like to eat.

A good friend of mine has cooked up a trip for himself and his wife, leaving by ship from New York and going through the Mediterranean to Greece and Crete and Italy . . . about seven or eight ports in about 18 days. I would like a trip like that. In fact, I may try to talk Vi out of the other trip . . . it's too damned expensive. The Mediterranean one is $2500 or $3000 apiece, so that's more my speed.

Our money comes from investments along the line, three pensions . . . the Fire Department, the track and Social Security. I didn't qualify for Social Security until I went to work for the race track, because firemen and policemen are not on it. And we have made investments here and there, and some of them are pretty good. And, as I say, we made some money at the race track. . . .

My only health deficiencies are from the fires I've been to and the volumes of smoke I've had to eat. In my day they had very poor masks, and we went into smoking buildings with nothing most of the time. Quite a few times I've been into atmospheres that were very toxic. It didn't bother me at the time, but as I grew older, I found that I could do less, and now I don't do anything in the way of a lot of physical exertion. After playing with my dog for five minutes, that's it. But other than that, I'm pretty healthy. I don't exercise. I guess I'm just too lazy. I tell myself I should, but every type of exercise that I like . . . basketball, tennis . . . I don't have the wind any more. The few exercises that I could do, I'm just too lazy to do. I've gotten by so far without them. I don't have too much of a weight problem, but I'm beginning to thicken up a little bit now.

But I come from a pretty long-lived family. My mother died at 64 of diabetes, and my father died at 69 of cancer, but there were quite a few of my family that lived a long time. Most of them run in their 80's. My brother ran down the family tree, and he dug up some relatives that I never knew about. They were in their 90's . . . 92 . . . 93. The only uncle I ever saw lived to 84. At 84 he had all of his teeth. He had at one time worn glasses, but he seemingly got his second eyesight and after awhile he discarded them. He was vigorous. I never saw him walk slow in his life. He was 83 at the time he met some woman at church. He talked to my mother about her, but he didn't get any encouragement from her at all. I remember my mother saying, "There's no fool like an old fool." But he married her, and I guess married life was a little too much for the guy. His wife was 40. He died a year later at 84, but he died happy.

Vi and I are Science of Mind people. As such, we have seen things, and our friends have gone through things, that have convinced us beyond all question that there's a life after death. But I haven't seen enough of this life yet. . . . Why be afraid of death when you're going on to another phase of life? So why fight it? Death doesn't mean a thing. The only thing is I don't want to die miserably. I nearly burned up once, I've been in an explosion once . . . I've been in a tough crack two or three times, and I didn't want to end that way. . . .

I think now, I would have been much different as a youngster. No one could ever turn me away from finishing school, because, to my mind, that's very important. I used to have an inferiority complex because my mother, father, sister and brother were college graduates, and I'm the only one that wasn't. But, in my lifespan I have a lot to be grateful for, and

I did just as well as lots of people I knew that had everything I wished I had at the time. And right now, I'm in as good shape as any of them.

The only thing I'd do different is that I wouldn't be such an ornery cuss. Perhaps that would have changed my whole life. Of course, nowadays, it's far different from what it was then. Just imagine yourself, for instance, if someone told you at the age of, say, 12, that there's no need to go to school, because when you get out, all you could be is a pullman porter, like my father was, or a waiter or shoe shine person, or, at the very best, a janitor . . . and you know they're telling you the truth. Largely, but not altogether, now you can go where your ability takes you. I know I'm grateful for being in my position, considering how it was when I started out.

(What I felt most strongly while interviewing Pat, was comfort . . . his and mine. He was very easy to interview. His relationship with Vi felt comfortable. The chairs in the living room of their house were easy to sit on. Pat likes to travel, but not if it involves the bustle of airports, so he now travels by boat. He loves going to the races, but not if it means driving 60 miles to get there, so he goes only to the nearby tracks. The phrase he used to describe his attitude towards death . . . "So why fight it?" . . . says a great deal about his attitude towards life. Why fight it?

The interview with Pat was the only one that ended because I ran out of tapes. We had talked far longer than I had expected or planned for. It was just plain comfortable talking with him. I'm sure that it was his comfort with himself that contributed so heavily to mine.)

7

If I Had It to Do Over Again,
I Wouldn't Change Anything

(Vivian, 72, is Taylor's wife of 49 years. She too looks far younger than her age.)

I think it's interesting to be interviewed. It's nice to be asked and to have the opportunity to have someone write about you. I've always been interested in writing. Several times I started classes at University Extension, but Pat was in the Fire Department, and the nights he wasn't home, I wasn't too happy about going out, so I didn't continue. But I've always liked the field of advertising and publicity, so I guess that's a part of the reason I like writing. My father and two uncles were all printers, and my dad used to say that printers ink ran in my blood. The field always had a certain appeal to me. I guess the reason I didn't follow it was that I got involved in the field of accounting.

One of my first jobs was in cost accounting, but I didn't know a thing about it when I applied. All I knew about was the difference between a debit and a credit. The man who interviewed me asked if I knew cost accounting, and I said, "Oh, yes." So I got the job. And after I was there three months, his accountant came to him and said "You don't need me any more. Vi can handle the books." I kept at it and I got so that at the end of another month I could make out the financial statements.

Another place I worked had just installed some new bookkeeping machines just before I came there. Two or three

49

weeks after that, the girl who operated the machines called in sick, and she didn't come back to work at all. So I said to the boss, "I can operate those machines." And he said, "Put that junk in the wastebasket and get over there." They really needed me, because, you see, everything was on a cash basis. They had no receivables. Everything was payables, and a lot of their money was made discounting their payables. They took advantage of every day . . . 10 days or 30th of the month terms. Every day of the month I paid bills. The 10th of the month sometimes I'd write 500 to 1,000 checks.

I think I got the feel for business from my father and two uncles. As I said, one uncle worked for a publishing company, and I've often told Pat, as a youngster growing up, I had books the minute they came off the press. So, reading has always been important to me. Right now . . . and for the past ten years . . . I've been interested in reading books on metaphysics. In fact, I've always been interested in psychic phenomena, and I've had some very interesting things happen to me.

There was one Sunday morning around nine o'clock that I said to Pat, "Honey, why don't you give your brother a call?" We had been planning to visit him and his wife in San Antonio. So Pat got on the phone to tell them we were coming, but his brother couldn't come to the phone because he was sick. His stomach had been upset for a couple of weeks. So when I insisted that Pat call, it was the first time that he knew his brother was sick in bed.

The next Sunday after that, I said to Pat, "Honey, I think you ought to give your brother another call." "Oh no," he said. "He's not all that sick. If he isn't alright, he'll call me. Nothing's gonna happen to him. I wish you'd stop worrying me about it. I'll call him next weekend." The next day, while I was fixing breakfast, the phone rang, and Pat answered it and said, "Oh, hey, how are you doing? . . . Okay . . . Okay . . . if I'm not here, Vi will be. Let us know right away." His brother was already *in* surgery. Pat looked at me and said, "You know, you tried every way you could to get me to call."

I think the thing that got me started in metaphysics . . . you see, I was brought up as a Methodist, and we were a fairly religious family. In fact, my father at one time wanted to be a minister, but I think that my mother felt she'd rather he had a steady income, so he didn't go any farther. And I was married in the church. But anyway, this one time I did something . . . I don't remember what it was . . . and I knew my mother was going to annihilate me for it. My mother was short, but her word was law, and you obeyed her orders or your life was in danger. So, out the back door I flew, over to my grandmother's house, Grandma wasn't in, but a friend of hers who was visiting her from Chicago came out and said, "Vivian, come in here! What's the matter?" I said, "Ohhhh, Mama's gonna kill me!" I told her what happened and she told me to sit down, I sat down on a stool and she taught me the first verse of Unity's Prayer of Faith: "God is my help in every need / God does my every hunger feed / God walks beside me and guides my way / Through every moment of the day." She told me to keep saying that all the way home. "But what's Momma gonna do," I wailed? And she said, "She isn't going to do anything." And she didn't! And I think that's where I started to believe in metaphysics.

I'll give you an example of why I believe in it so strongly. When my friend Eva and her little girl were staying with us, she came down one morning and said to me, "Vi, something happened last night and I'm afraid to tell Pat." I asked her what it was and she said, "His mother appeared." This was after his mother died, you understand. So I asked her what she looked like, and she said, "Well, she was standing at the foot of the bed, and I could see her outline. She had her hair down over one eye, and she said to tell Taylor to read the Psalms." Now, Eva had never seen my mother-in-law, not even a picture, and yet she described her perfectly. And my mother-in-law was the only person who ever called Pat by his real name, Taylor!

The other thing . . . you know we go to the races. Well, I have dreamed daily doubles right out of the picture. The first time, I dreamed my father gave me a birthday party, and I could hear the music and the people moving down this hall, and there's this big disc with the number 21 on it. I told Pat,

"Honey, I dreamed 21. I'm going to the track to play it." In the first race the number 2 horse came in and paid over $60, and in the second race the number 1 horse came in and paid 60 some dollars too. And the daily double paid $2700!

I've always loved horses . . . all my life. I just thought they were the most beautiful animals, and to be able to go to the track to see them run. . . . But I got to like the betting aspect too. I started studying . . . you know, you have to like figures to study the racing form. You've got money, weight, speed . . . everything to take into consideration. Pat even bought me a calculator to take with me when we go. I've got several systems. No one system works everywhere all the time. You've got different tracks, different types of weather, different times of the year, and I have systems to cover them. And we're ahead of the game. Oh, there's some years we really make it, and others we don't do so good, but we'll make up for it later at another track or another meet. And every time we decide to go on a trip, I've made the money to go.

I would travel at the drop of a hat . . . any place, any time. I love it! I wasn't born for staying around and doing housework. I could spend all day . . . all week, just going from the top of the house to the bottom, but I think there's more to life than keeping house. I think it's important to keep a nice house, and I like nice things, but when I was working, I paid someone to do it. But this every day cooking. . . . I prefer paper plates to washing dishes. And Pat looks pretty good for 49 years of my cooking.

I met Pat while I was going with a fellow who later became president of Golden West Life Insurance Co. I went with him to a fraternity dance. I was standing there talking to a girl friend and who should I see across the hall but his royal highness. I asked who he was and she said, "Don't you know him? That's *the* Taylor Patterson." You see, his family was very prominent, and he was quite the eligible young man at the time . . . and very handsome. The fellow I was going with introduced me to him, and we started dancing. Afterwards, the fellow said it was the stupidest thing he'd ever done when he introduced me to Pat. So, we saw each other from time to time, and we just started going together. And we were married in '29. Pat was . . . let's see . . . 28, and I was 22.

I wanted to have children, but I couldn't, and I guess that's why I've devoted so much of my life to raising someone else's. I raised Pat's sister's children. I've always loved kids, and we both loved girls, so we've been raising all the girls we could find to raise. And if I had it to do over again, I wouldn't change anything.

I think that part of the reason that Pat and I have gotten along so well is due to the fact that I had the most marvelous mother-in-law. She and I were very close. We took in plays together and we'd go to dinner together. She was a person who cared about me. She told me that most important things about living with her son . . . how to get along with him. To me, that was most valuable. Oh, we've had our differences and then some, but basically they were around money. You see, I had been used to working with large sums of money, and there were many times I spent my paycheck, charging things before I even got home. So, if I didn't get to the mailbox soon enough and he got the bill for what I had spent, then there was an argument. But that was the only thing we argued about. There was always the underlying feeling that he was the one that I wanted to be with . . . that he was my choice.

You know, a lot of women have problems with their husbands' being under foot when they retire, but I've been attuned to it. You see, the major portion of our married life was when Pat was with the Fire Department, with 24 hours on and 48 off, or 24 on and 24 off, with five days in a row off every three months, or something like that. So I was accustomed to his being home more than many husbands who work at 9 to 5 jobs. And sometimes, when I was at work, and he was home, he'd call me and ask me how busy I was, and could I come home early so we could take in a show or something.

You see, I worked steadily for 20 years after we were first married. After that, I worked for a company where I went out on assignments, and if I didn't want to, I didn't have to. It sort of dovetailed with Pat's time, you know, because I could be off and at home when he was at home. That was always the most important thing to me. So we looked forward to the day when we would be together more and do the things we wanted. But he wasn't home that long before he went to work for the race track. And then, we were both working! I mean I was working the track every day I could.

When his sister first heard what we were doing after he retired, she said, "You mean you've got my brother going to the track?" I said to her, "I've got your brother living!" You see, when he quit the Fire Department, he was kind of at a loss. He had so much free time to do what he wanted to do. But you can only do so much, and then what? People may say they want to retire because they're tired of the routine, but it's the routine that keeps them alive. You have to have some kind of interest that keeps you moving. I'm on him all the time to do something or go someplace, and we get in the biggest arguments, but who has the best time of anybody there? . . .

One of our neighbors is a fireman, and whenever he sees me, he asks, "How's the Captain?" I tell him that the Captain's fine, and he says that the Captain looks fine, but I tell him that it's the Captain's wife that keeps him that way. It's one thing to say all that we do is go to the races, but that's what keeps him going. That keeps him active. If you don't do anything but decide which chair you're going to sit in, Mother Nature has a way of moving you out.

At our age, we'd be very stupid if we didn't think of survivors. I think that a lot of people put their heads in their pillows when it comes to facing these things. You see, the 37 years that Pat was with the Department, there were fires and things, and I was facing that all along. And I had to know which way I would go. We talk about it frequently. Pat says I should sell the house when he passes. I don't know about that, but I'll tell you this . . . I've got ideas about what to do. I would be interested in taking classes in metaphysics, and I will, if he dies before I do.

Besides, death isn't the end. It couldn't be. When I was just a youngster, and my mother's sister died, I wondered where they had room to bury all the people that kept dying. But now, I have the conviction . . . and some people might think it's hogwash . . . there's too much mystery attached to death. To me, the body is through, and the consciousness moves on to another sphere of activity. And that's all there is to it.

(Vi impressed me as a woman who immersed herself in whomever and whatever she cared about. Pat's well being, she made very clear, is her first priority, but she has more than enough energy left for the activities that interest her . . . travelling, figuring the odds on the horses, studying metaphysics. The things that don't interest her . . . like washing dishes . . . get short shrift.

She was soft-spoken; at times her voice level was so low that I had trouble picking it up on my tape recorder. But the determination in her voice came through loud and clear. There was no question in my mind that she will do what she has to and wants to do to enjoy the rest of her life, if Pat predeceases her.

A fragment of our conversation at the end of the interview added a dimension to what I had already seen of her positive outlook on life: Everyone I had spoken to while working on the book said he hoped I could get it published . . . except Vi. She said, "I just know you're going to.")

8
I'm a Fighter.
I'm Not Ready to Give Up.

*(Morrie Rabin is the active president of the
Santa Clara County City of Hope Volunteer
Auxiliary. He was introduced to me by a friend
who is the accountant for the agency.)*

I was born in Poland, and I'm 88 years old. I want to say to
you that I was an orphan at three . . . that is, my father died
when I was three. I didn't even know him until my mother
showed me when . . . before the funeral. She took me over to
him and said, "This is your father." This is the only time I
seen him. He was dealing in horses and I never seen him. My
mother was very poor. Let me just say to you, as poor as my
mother was, she gave me the best care. She would see to it that
I had fresh milk. In the village where I was born, my relatives
were rich . . . they had a cow to themselves. My mother ordered
me to go there for milk. She gave me 10 groschen I should pay
for it. So, one day, I came back with the 10 groschen. She said
to take it right back. "If they don't take the 10 groschen, leave
the milk there." She was so independent and she didn't want
anything to be gotten for nothing. . . . But I was happy. My
mother took very good care of me, but let me say to you, when
you're born in a poor home, you don't know what you're
missing. . . . My mother died in the first World War from
hunger. There wasn't enough to eat. She gave the bread she
was allowed to eat to children.

My mother wanted to bring me up the right way. Up

until I was 12 years old she held me in Cheder while she was trying to make a living for herself. Then she said she wanted me to be a rabbi, but I said, "Mother, you're too poor to even keep me in Cheder. I have to go to work." But she said, "You don't know anything. How can you go to work?" I said that her father was a tailor and I could be one too. So she gave me away for three years, and I learned the trade.

After that, I left home and went to another village near Warsaw and worked a year . . . they paid by the year with room and board. When the year was over, I went to Warsaw and got myself a job in a tailoring store. That was about . . . oh, I was about 16 years old, and my mother was already talking to me that I should leave Russia. Poland at that time still belonged to Russia. She said, "I don't want you to go into the Czar's army." So I said, "Where can I go?" She said "Paris is good enough. It's not too far away." So, at 17 years I went to Paris. But before that I was already a union man. In Warsaw, there was a great demand for unions, and the minute I was working at a machine where the workers were organized, they took me into the union. The union had social significance. We had lectures, and they were trying to make a Socialist out of me. . . . When I left for Paris, they gave me a transfer to the Syndicate in Paris.

The first job I got there was not a union shop, and the Syndicate pressed me I should organize that shop. There came a time when the boss changed the hours. He said, "When you come to work, you can't come anymore at seven o'clock in the morning. You'll have to come at 8:30." Nobody wanted to start that late and finish at six o'clock at night. So I thought that's the chance for me to get them into the union. I told them, "I think you have a good reason to strike," and I brought them in. The strike didn't last very long, and everybody went back. So I went to the foreman and said, "You know, I think you realize that I wanted to do something but I failed, and now you could tell me to go. You don't have to keep me." He said, "Well, now you know the rights of the people not to belong to a union. I like your work, and I want you to stay." I thought that was a very good idea, and I didn't lose my job.

When I was 21, I received a card from America. The union there said I should come . . . there was jobs there and they would pay my way and I should come immediately. So, so long as I didn't have to pay my fare . . . but, you see I was already married since I was 19. . . . My wife was also coming from Warsaw, and we used to be together for about two or three years. She also was a member of the union, and then she came to Paris and we were married. . . . So I told my wife "The card is just for myself. You'll have to remain here till I get there, and then I'll bring you over." And in three months, I sent her a card to come with the child. We already had a child . . . a year old.

When I got here to America, the first day that I went to look for a job, I seen an advertisement "Operator-Pocketmaker is wanted." I was just one day in America when I went for that job. I never worked an electric machine before and when they put me down to work, I started trying it. It didn't work because the switch was off. And when the switch went on, I realized I had to take my foot off, because it was running away. . . . Why were they so patient with me? I found out later that I was scabbing on people that were out on strike. So I left the job. I was too much of a union-conscious man.

So that was 1912. In 1912, I got myself a job as a pocket maker in Brooklyn. The shop was working from five o'clock in the morning until about eight or nine o'clock at night. The religious Jews was putting on their tallis and tfillin to pray before they could have a bit to eat. That was how it was when we started. But by the end of 1912 we went out on strike, and we struck for about three months. I went out on strike with about $3.00 in my pocket . . . that's all I had. All right . . . the union provided some meals, and we struggled. Finally they settled the strike, and when I came back the first day, the boss says, "Must I keep you here if I don't want you?" I said, "What's wrong with me? Is my work bad?" And he said, "It's not your work. You're too big of a union man. If not for you, my shop would not be in the union."

I worked for awhile on the Executive Board of the union, but then my wife got sick and we had to go to Los Angeles. She had lung trouble, and Los Angeles was a warm climate. So, in 1920 we moved there with my children. We had one daughter and we had also one boy. And I was doing very well until my wife died.

Before I married again, it was hard to raise the children, and I needed some help. My second wife, I met in Los Angeles . . . between friends . . . and we've been married 55 years already. . . . The Communist Party had some schools that took in children, and I got the boy in there. The reason I bring the boy in is when the Spanish Civil War broke out, he went to Spain with the Lincoln Brigade. He died there. He was a good boy.

After that, a friend in San Francisco . . . he was the manager of the union there . . . he said, "Come, I got a job for you." I worked a lot of different jobs there. . . . In 1929, I was a little farmer in Petaluma raising chicks. And when everybody else was closing down because chicks wasn't selling too good, the feeding company came . . . you see, I owed them $2000 . . . and wants to know are we going to stay or we going to close down. I said to them, "I'm a fighter. I'm not ready to give up. I'm going to stay." Since the chicks weren't marketing too good, my wife took care of them, and I got a job. So every cent I paid them off.

Not long after that, the General Strike in San Francisco with the Longshoremen took place. I was active in that. And I was later elected to the Executive Board of my union. You see, I had a name of being a left winger. And in 1945 . . . no, '46, I got a letter to come up to the president of the union. The business agent left to take a foreman's job and he recommended that I should take over his job until there should be an election. That was right after the war that I became business agent, and I stayed with them until '63.

The workers depend on you. They can't fight because they're working. They depend on the business agent to be a diplomat and in the meantime to see to it that they get a little better wage. That's their living. That's why I was re-elected six times for three years. As a matter of fact, I was already 73 and they wanted me to stay. They had a law you should retire at 65, but I always got a letter from the president that I should stay. So I said enough is enough. But the president was a Navy man and he got a letter saying that he should come and serve six months, so he says, "You can't retire now. You'll retire when I come back." When he came back, I retired. They made me a banquet, and I'm retired for 15 years now.

While I was working as a business agent, we were invited to Duarte to visit the City of Hope hospital. You see, my first wife died there. I promised if I'll retire, I'll be very active in it. We organized an auxiliary for the City of Hope, and for the past 10 years I am president of the Santa Clara Auxiliary. And this is not the only activity we do. We are also members of Histadrut. We pay regular dues yearly. My wife is a member of the Pioneer Women, but it's a little hard for her to get to the meetings, so I go with her to them. We don't have a car.

You see, I only got one good eye. This other one doesn't work so good. On the 29th of next month I'm going to the hospital for a cataract removal. You see, in September, I'll be 89, and, knock on wood, I'm doing alright except for that one eye. I only see a little bit out of it. . . .

When I was a business agent, it was a nervous, nervous job, and I smoked. But I started getting trouble with my ears, so I went to the doctor. He says, "Not to worry about your ears. Only stop smoking and that'll go away." So I promised him the minute I'll retire, I'll stop. And I did. I stopped like that, and I didn't take a cigarette since. Not at all. There's one thing about me . . . once I undertake something, I'll do it.

I'm alright. I just live natural. I have a big yard, and I keep it in order. I have a pump for my own water. I have some fruit trees . . . what do you call them? . . . almonds. Sometimes I take the almonds off the tree, peel them and dry them, and send them to my grandson. He likes almonds. . . . My daughter lives in the house right behind me, and she's a widow, so I'm a little busy on both sides, taking care of her place as much as I can. She doesn't want me to do anything. As a matter of fact, she doesn't even want me to go to the grocery by myself and push the little wagon. I go with her shopping every Saturday. So together is not so bad. And now that my wife is getting a little older, I can't leave her in the house by herself. She goes out for a walk, gets lost, and we have to look for her. But she just joined the City of Hope, and I take her with me when I go.

We have lots of friends. When we go to the Histadrut, everybody knows us there. Whenever there's a candidate for raising money, we go. We also buy Israel Bonds every once in awhile if it's possible. The people in my wife's Pioneer Women all know us there. They're an older bunch, but a little younger than we are. They're retired from the unions. I go to their meetings, but I can't go too often because I'm busy with the City of Hope. So I could only participate so much and no more. . . . We get along nicely.

We're active in Jewish organizations, but I'm not too religious. I was raised in religion until I was 12 years old, and my mother wanted me to be a rabbi. But after that I was kinda taken in with unions . . . left wing unions. But I'm a Jew. And right now I'm very much for Israel. And to the Histadrut, I help all I can. Maybe some people don't like to hear that I'm not so religious, but that's the truth. . . .

When I say we live natural . . . our meals are very plain. We sleep the regular time. We don't drink, we don't smoke . . . the both of us. We try to do the best to keep healthy. And if I have to do some work in the yard, I can still do it. If a tree is loose, I could lay it down and saw it and chop it up.

I do all the cooking. In the morning . . . fruit, toast, eggs, and tea . . . no coffee . . . cottage cheese for lunch with fruit, toast, and a drink. I always have meat or chicken for dinner. And vegetables with all our dinners. Not only it's plain food, it's healthier to digest. It works better with us. We are doing very well.

I read a lot, and time rolls very fast with me. You see, knock on wood, I sleep very well. I get rested, and I could do a lot of things. We get up around 6:30 and my wife gets ready for her walks. I help her out to see that she gets out alright. I make my exercises, so I don't go with her. But when the family gets together, my daughters and I all go for a walk in the park.

We cover about four miles. I'm a very good walker. . . . After that, we eat breakfast and we read a little bit. About 11:30 we eat lunch. Then we start reading again. I've got a couple of chores in the garage . . . here and there fixing to do. I'm the plumber, the electrician . . . I'm a little bit of everything. Maybe I'm not so fast on it, but I learn it as I do it. And when you go buy parts, they tell you how to do it anyhow. In the beginning I used to paint the house, but now I decided I'm going to pay for it. It's getting a little too big for me. . . . And about 3:30 or 4:00 I'm beginning to make dinner. After dinner, we read, listen to the news or a program on television. We go to sleep about nine o'clock.

You know, I went all through my life in struggle, but I came out ahead of it. I'm healthy, and I'm not afraid to die when I reach that age. You see, coming out of a poor family like ours, my preparation for life wasn't too good. The only thing I see now is when I was 57 and became a business agent, I got a steady salary for close to 17 years. I didn't expect it, but it came out that way. I feel that this alone gave me a push in life. What I'm trying to say is that the trade I was in, the jobs were never steady. We had to struggle. Today you worked, and you could just make ends meet, but you get laid off when there is a slack month or two or three, and it wasn't too good. But when you get a job in a union that holds you for 17 years, you feel you're secure with a living. Although the wage wasn't too high, you know at the end you'll get a little pension. And Social Security, thanks God to Roosevelt, helps you out quite a bit. I'm doing alright . . . Social Security is $322 and my pension check is about $280. And the house is paid for. I bought it for cash out of my earnings. We're doing fine.

What interests me now I would like to see the whole world should be a little better than it is. I would like Israel should be free and make peace with her neighbors. For once, the Jewish people have a homeland. They never had before, and I'd like to see that they get along very good.

(I sent Morrie a transcript of the tape and I visited him at his home a month after the interview to see if he wanted to make

any changes in it. Other than a date or two, there was nothing he wanted to correct, and we were both pleased with the way he came across in the interview. While there, I asked him to sign a release, authorizing me to use the material for research or possible publication when I finished. To my surprise, he was very emphatic about not wanting to sign until I was done; he said he'd do it then. I stammered something like, "But Morrie, it may take a year or two, and you may be dead when I'm ready to use it." "Oh no," he said, "I'll be around."

I came back about a year later, and, as he said he would be, he was around, and he signed the release. Nothing describes the battler in Morrie better than that exchange about his signature.)

9
The Important Thing Is to Love People

(I met Elizabeth Farrell *through my across-the-street neighbor. I was told that I might have difficulty in setting up an interview with her because she was so often and unpredictably in pain. Liz, as she insisted I call her, is 72 and lives in a Senior Citizens housing project in Daly City.)*

I was born out in the country near a small town north of Chico on August third, 1906. My dad was an itinerant minister. He was self-educated, and we had a large family . . . eight of us children plus my mother's half brothers and sisters. We were poor as church mice, because my dad gave so much away to other people. When I was a child, I didn't have all those good feelings that my mother and father tried to imbue us with. They felt they had to share. It was years before I forgave my mother for giving away a pink dress of mine. I had this new dress . . . I was eight years old, and I managed to earn some money to get this pink seersucker dress with a pink sash around it. And there was this very, very poor girl that lived close to us, and she needed a dress to graduate from the old country school we went to. Well, I came home one day and Mama was lengthening my beautiful pink dress for this tall scrawny neighbor girl. I cried and I had a conniption fit. Well, Dad came in from the outside where he was trying to get some vegetables planted, and he wanted to know what was going on. I sobbed, "Mama, I hate her! I hate her!" And, you know, my dad understood that. He picked me up and sat me down on his lap and told me how much better it was to give than to receive. But I didn't believe him for a minute, I was so angry with him.

I wasn't particularly happy as a child. I worried about everything . . . the whole world. And I didn't have enough loving from my mother, but, of course, I was prejudiced against her because she was the one who disciplined me. One discipline she inflicted on me was sewing, and I hated it. I wanted to be outside . . . in the air. I wanted to climb hills and wade the creek.

I wouldn't want to relive my childhood. I had three summers of being desperately ill from the malaria I got from the mosquitoes that were born in all the irrigation ponds. I had temperatures that ran to 106 degrees at times, and the enlarged spleen I've got today is on account of that. And then there was the stress of growing up, being poor, and never having the nice clothes that other kids had. I started working very early, helping my brother-in-law feed his poultry. I'd work from as soon as school got out in the summer to the fall, and I earned enough money to buy a few clothes. Fact of the matter is that's how I earned that pink dress that my mother lengthened for that poor kid. . . .

I got through school early. I was only 11 years old when I graduated from grammar school. I think that's because I started to read when I was about four years old. My dad subscribed to the *Call-Bulletin* in San Francisco, and I would sit on his lap and read with him. Of course, I learned to read the Bible . . . we were compelled to do that. Of all the girls . . . there were seven girls and one boy . . . I was the one most given to reading, because I was the tail end of the family and there were no playmates for me out in the country. So I turned to reading. I read all the books in my father's library. I was reading Thackeray and Dickens by the time I was seven or eight years old.

I was reaching out for so many things . . . the things I didn't understand about the evolution of nature and what was

happening in the world. I wasn't particularly interested in
boys, but I knew about sex because we had animals on the
farm and it came naturally. I didn't have to be told about those
things. Although later on when my dad could see that the boys
were attracted to me, he talked to me, and he told me what
could happen and how it would be possible for me to very
easily get impregnated. My mother wouldn't talk to me about
that, but my dad talked to all of us girls, and he prided himself
that there were no shotgun weddings in our family.

When I was 22 I fell head over heels in love with a man
who owned the newspaper I was working for in Chico. He
was forty-something and he was married, but his wife was not
with him very much of the time and their marriage was
breaking up. He was a very intelligent and gentle person. He
was a musician as well as a newspaperman, and he taught me
all there was to know about the business. I operated the
machines, I did the editorials, and then later I started report-
ing news. I think I loved him so deeply because he was a father
image for me.

We got married after his divorce, and pretty soon I began
to realize how ignorant I was. I thought I knew all about the
world from reading. I didn't have much education although I
always wanted more. I guess I didn't have the discipline to
apply myself to it. My husband helped me . . . he showed me
books and he started me reading in religion. We used to get
books from the little library in Chico, and we'd order others
from the library in Sacramento. And I began to achieve a
certain amount of poise and began doing things in that little
town. I helped establish a woman's club, I was on the Board of
the Salvation Army, and I taught Sunday School for awhile,
until I started questioning the divinity of Christ.

I told that to my dad. I told him I couldn't bring myself to
believe that Christ was divine or that it was God who impregnated Mary, and he said, "You may just have something there,
kid." He never questioned anything I came to believe. He
really mellowed.

I had the best part of my dad. He and my husband were
very close to each other. Years before, my father would never

have thought of going to a ball game on Sunday, but later he would get into his dinkey little Ford every time he could, drive over to have dinner with us, and we'd go to a game. It was delightful. I had the sunset years with my dad.

He was killed in an automobile accident when he was 74 years old. He was coming home from Grange, and he missed a turn in the road. When I lost my dad, I didn't know what I was going to do. I thought I would die. For a long time, though, I couldn't shed a tear for him. But I'd wake up with nightmares, crying . . . I was trying to get to him and I couldn't. My husband used to hold me in his arms and comfort me during those times.

We never had any children. He didn't want me to have any, but I always wanted to, because I was always used to having so many around. But he didn't want to share our life with a child and he felt very strongly about it. I don't know whether he was troubled about the history of mental illness in his family, because he never told me about it until he himself became mentally ill.

You see, he had hardening of the arteries and it affected his brain, and he started losing his mind. He became prematurely senile and he had periods of violence. He finally got to the point that I had to commit him to Napa State Hospital . . . I still have quite a bit of trouble talking about it . . . I used to drive down once a month to see him, and it was the most agonizing thing . . . to see someone so brilliant, so talented in so many ways . . . to see his whole personality change. But he had periods of violence, and I couldn't do anything about them.

While I was visiting, I met a man whose wife was in Napa at the same time my husband was. I'd visit my husband and he's visit his wife. And we used to have a picnic on the lawn with his two kids. We developed a romance . . . we turned to each other. My family didn't understand it and neither did his, but we needed each other so desperately.

That was a long time ago, and my husband died in the hospital, and his wife died in childbirth later on, but I still see him once in awhile. He would like . . . well, let's put it this way . . . he's sexually active for a man who's 72 years old. He jogs, he flies a plane, he plays golf, and . . . oh, he's the handsomest thing you'd ever want to lay eyes on, and I just think he's a delightful person. I enjoy him very much, but my days of wine and roses are over, and I don't want to spoil my memories. You know, there's a saying that someone told me and it fits me pretty well, I think: I've never been a wanton woman, but I've never been a woman in want of men.

I remarried once and it was awful, just awful. He was an alcoholic and I didn't know it. I was a friend of his wife's, and they were going through a very bad time, and he started drinking, but I didn't know that. After their divorce, he started courting me in the old fashioned way, with flowers and everything, and I thought he must be a pretty fine man. But then . . . oh, it was awful. One time he tried to kill me and he nearly did. So I divorced him, and that was the end of my marriages. No more! That was it!

When I lived at a hotel before I moved here, there was another man living there, and we had wonderful communication. We delved into religions and lots of things like that. He was born in Hongkong and I called him my guru. He's rather small and he's somewhat older than I am, but I love him and he loves me. I don't see much of him, because he only comes to see me once in awhile, but I never talk to him for any length of time but what my mind just expands. It's like taking LSD, I guess. I always have so much that I want to ask him about. After all this time, he still calls me a couple of times a week.

There was one evening I was all tied up in knots. I went through three nights of not sleeping, and I was literally pacing the floor. I was in pain, walking with a crutch and a cane . . . walking . . . walking . . . walking. I just couldn't get comfortable in any position. But I had read so much about people getting hooked on drugs, and Lord knows, there were so many people living at that old hotel that were addicted. I asked myself, was I going to be like that? So I just stopped taking my Valium or any medication, just like that. But I was in pain.

Well, I didn't come down to breakfast two mornings in a

row, and I didn't come down to dinner, and this man friend, my guru, began to worry about me, so he came to my room to ask me what was wrong. I said, "I don't know. I'm just scared to death." And he talked to me for a long time, and he made me believe I could overcome the pain. He taught me self-hypnosis and it really helped me.

So now, if my brain doesn't crack, I'm really going to manage quite well. I had a time about six or eight months ago when I developed a growth here in my abdomen, and I still have it. And then my spleen . . . remember I told you about those mosquitoes and the malaria when I was growing up? . . . my spleen is so enlarged where this bowel presses on it. The doctor said I should have a biopsy done on it, but I said I didn't want it, because I didn't want to be cut up. You see, I hadn't kept up with modern medicine so I didn't realize that they just go in with a little hollow needle. So they did the biopsy, and it turned out to be a benign growth of some kind . . . not a tumor. It was about a month before I knew that I didn't have cancer. It almost blew my mind, because there's something so horrendous about cancer.

Oh, I have osteoarthritis in my ankles that makes it a little tough for me to get around, but I got some accupuncture treatment from this fellow who was teaching it at U.C. Hospital in San Francisco. And I was so free of pain for awhile that I felt like jumping up and cracking my heels together. It was on account of the pain that I had to retire. You see, I was working as a nurse companion, but I just couldn't function any more.

Fact of the matter is, I was feeling so good after that accupuncture that I went on a trip to my high school reunion. It was a bad, wet day, and this young man, the driver, hit a truck, and the tail end of it jackknifed. I fractured my collarbone, and I landed on the arm of the seat right next to my coccyx, and it fractured three vertebrae. I landed in the hospital again, and they put me in traction. It was the most awful thing! I told them I wasn't going to stay in traction but the nurse said I had to. I said, "Well, I'm going to start screaming until you get me out of this thing." She wasn't going to, so I just started screaming the place down, and they took me out of it. . . . Anyway, my health is excellent, other than that. I can go to places, and with a little help I can start getting more exercise. But it still is difficult for me to walk.

Of course, I can't work any more. I had kept the newspaper going for quite some time and I made a go of it. But then I sold it to be nearer to my husband in the hospital and to pay off the hospital bills. The young man I sold it to went bust. Afterwards I had a good job here in San Francisco managing a dress shop. The last of my working days was as a nurse, which was very fortunate for me because that's how I got qualified for Social Security.

I don't know what I'd do without Social Security; it's all I have for an income. I get what's called SSI . . . Supplemental Security Income . . . and it's $312 a month. That's my whole income, and it's all I can do to manage. Every once in awhile, of course, I do get a little check in the mail from my relatives, for which I'm very grateful. The rent is $150, and out of the $312, believe it or not, I manage to put some by for a rainy day, and I have almost $550 or $600 in the bank, so that if they raise the rent, like they're talking about, I can survive.

I don't know if I'm that unique from these poor creatures who live in this project, but I do think that I'm able to keep my equilibrium. I think it's mind over matter. Of course, I don't have the same kind of faith that some of these people around here who ache so much of the time . . . some of these born-again-Christians. They get to praying and telling me that prayer will overcome anything, and that I should try it for my arthritis. Well, I know damn well it's not going to, so I just settle down and out-think the pain. And then I get to reading.

You know, I don't think there's anything can happen to me now, except my being completely incapacitated to the point where I can't control my bodily functions. I think that too many things have happened to me, and I think I can overcome whatever comes. I think I have the serenity to do that. Oh, I get madder than blue blazes some time, but I have a certain amount of serenity, and I certainly have a love of life. I don't know how to tell you I arrived at it, except that I think that grief and pain do one of two things for you. It makes you a better person or else it makes you a mean so-and-so. I have sworn to myself that I'm not going to get mean, if I can avoid it.

And I'm not afraid of dying. Why, we start dying the day we're born. I came to grips with that, because I nearly died a few times. I truly believe that I haven't had time on this earth to finish . . . there's so much I would like to follow through with. I wish I could help people . . . I wish that there was some way I could be able to bring general peace around. There are so many starving and ill-fed people in this world. There's so much violence. Some day, I think I'll come back and say to you, "Look, I was Liz Farrell when I was here before, and I've come back for another chance."

I think the important thing is to love people. I don't mean just to like people . . . you can't like them all. Some of them are so cruel and mean, but I don't get angry with them for their meanness . . . or if I do, I just think, well, I don't understand them. But to try to give love is about all I know how to say or do.

Every once in a while, there's an old gentleman that comes around here . . . he wants to be loved so badly. He had a beautiful relationship with a woman who died of cancer, and he's still seeking someone to live with him. I put my arms around him and love him. That's what he needs badly. He needs to be loved and have his halo shined a little bit . . . his wings burnished up. I'm always happy when he comes to see me. He says, "Whenever I get low, I just take the bus and come over to see you."

(Pain and suffering were, in my understanding, almost synonymous . . . that is, up to the time I met Liz Farrell. I learned from her that there was a big difference between the two. She had not chosen to be in pain, but she had chosen not to suffer. It was almost unbelievable hearing this woman with arthritic ankles, distended abdomen, and enlarged spleen saying, "my health is excellent, other than that." It became a little more believable when I heard her say a little later on, "I think pain and grief do one of two things for you. It makes you a better

person, or it makes you a mean so-and-so." Well, Liz is not a mean so-and-so. She has made her peace with pain. You don't know Liz unless you know that about her.

You also don't know her unless you know about her femininity. I felt that female warmth from the moment I met her. From what she told me about herself, I think many men have sensed that too. I know for sure that my wings felt burnished up when she hugged me and said goodbye.)

10

I'm Still Amazed That I've Lived This Long

(Elna Bannerman is my friend Dave's mother-in-law. I had never met her but she was described to me as a "real live wire." She is 89 and lives in the downstairs apartment of a building that her friend Vera owns, just outside of Walnut Creek.)

On just an ordinary day, I do one thing first unless I have to hurry. I enjoy reading the newspaper in the morning. That was a luxury I promised myself when I was working and didn't have time to do. And then I go to a Senior Citizens group over on Fourth Avenue. I've gone there on weekdays for five or six years now. But just last weekend, for the first time, I went to a group that meets right over the hill in the park two blocks from here. I knew it would be more convenient for me, so I just thought I'd try it and see, because I have to go on the bus and transfer to get to the one I've been going to all along. Then, my friend, Vera, and I love to play bridge. We have a loosely organized group that plays on Saturday nights. And we belong to another foursome from my church, and we meet intermittently. And I go to my church Guild and that sort of thing. It seems as if the days are gone before you know it. It's Monday morning and then it's Saturday night.

I have an awful time keeping up with my housekeeping or sewing a button and that sort of thing. And I watch television occasionally. I'm kind of a night owl, but I don't keep the television on all the time. I would rather read than listen to most of the programs. But then, I'm always behind in my reading too, and I don't get as much done as I'd like to. And, of course, Vera has lived here in Walnut Creek so much longer than I have and she has a wide circle of friends, and some of her friends have become my friends. On the whole, I would say, I have had a good life. I enjoy friends and people and having a good time, but I don't know anyone who's as old as I am.

I don't have any men friends now. . . . My husband and I celebrated our golden wedding anniversary thirteen years ago. He was somewhat older than I . . . not too much though. I think we met at one of the summer band concerts that they had around the city parks in St. Louis. There was one near us that we always went to, and he was there with some other boys that we knew. Of course, I was grown by that time, so everything went along . . . and we got married.

And then he wanted to go to Canada. So we went. It was a very interesting experience and I wouldn't give anything for those years . . . oh, the beautiful gardens we had! But it got to be that the long cold winters were just too much. He was about to conscripted into the Canadian Army, but, of course, he was an American citizen and he had a choice of going in with their forces or going back home. And since I would have been alone and my daughter Carol was a baby, we decided to come back to St. Louis.

And everything went along . . . The only real crisis we had was the Depression, which didn't prove to be a family crisis, but it was not good. Of course, people today have no recollection, no understanding of what it meant to people who had always been self-supporting and independent. And then to have their world just fall apart!

I tell the girls . . . Carol's girls . . . "There's nothing like just plain old money." The people who had money during the Depression made money, because they could buy anything they wanted to, because they had the cash to pay for it. There weren't too many who did, but there were some. Things were at rock bottom . . . that's when my husband and I bought our house. If we'd had more money we could have bought more property, but I suppose we were lucky to be able to buy one piece.

That house in St. Louis . . . well, it's been a Godsend to me because when I finally sold it, I got ten times as much as what we paid for it. I invested some of the money in a little Pacific Gas and Electric stock, and I have some money in Mutual Funds. I also have a few second mortgages that I've been fortunate to get into. I get 10% interest, but, from what I hear, I ought to get more. But if I get 10% regularly, I can make it. And, of course, there's Social Security. So, I'm not wealthy, but I'm on my own. I don't have assistance from anybody else.

Anyhow . . . when we got back home from Canada, my husband went into the garage business for . . . oh, about 15 years, until his health began to fail. It was that winter business that was so rough. The garage was full and emitting all that smoke, and he'd come home every night chilled to the bone. The doctor told him, "Bannerman, there's nothing else for it. You've got to get out of that business." So he did, and after that he started up a little tailoring business in one of the early shopping centers, and he did pretty well. I tell you that job saved his life, because he was in no shape to get a job from somebody else.

Of course, that was during the Depression, and I needed to get a job, particularly with Carol growing up and our wanting her to get on with her education. So I started to work for a friend, just doing some sewing for awhile. This friend and a couple of her friends had started a small custom professional garment business. There were five or six of us working in a little shop. And then I took an examination and went to work at City Hall. In my wildest dreams I had never thought of working there, because I knew about what some of those political machines had done to the city, and I definitely was opposed to it. I worked in the Assessor's Office, and I ended up there in charge of Personal Taxes with 20 or 30 people, mostly women, working for me at the time I retired.

I retired in '57, and my husband died shortly after that, but I stayed in St. Louis for four more years. And then Carol

. . . she and I had always been so close . . . well, she was living out here, and she said that she and her husband, David, would like to have me live with them, but that I would have to decide if and when I wanted to come. I have a very good friend who's a firm adherent of Christian Science, and I'll never forget what she wrote me. She said, "Elna, if this is right, everything will go smoothly and you'll sell your house right away." And, of course, I did, and everything just seemed to fall right into place. Of course, Carol's girls were out here too, both grown and with their own children, and so my family's all around me.

And then Carol died, and . . . those two years after she died were just terrible. It just seemed as if the bottom of everything dropped out. But David let me stay on with him, although I could have gone to live with Carol's daughters. But I would have been so completely strange there. Meantime I was making friends here, and I didn't want to give them up.

I struck up an immediate friendship with Vera. She's very outgoing and likes to do things. We went on a trip to Europe in 1971 before we had known each other too long. That was only a year after I had come out here. We just got the brochure and made the trip and it was marvelous. We're going on another one in a couple of months from now. Anyway, Carol had wanted us to get acquainted and she invited her over to dinner one night, and then Vera invited me over for lunch one day to play bridge with a few friends of hers, and from then on we've been very, very good friends.

This apartment I'm in belongs to Vera. Her husband had used this downstairs part of their home for his engraving business, but it had stood vacant for several years after he died and she had sold the business. And after Carol died, she said to me, "The downstairs room would certainly make a nice apartment for someone, but I don't want a stranger in my house." And she asked me if I'd be interested in making a change. I said that I was, and she said, "Would you like it if I fixed up the place?" Well, I said I'd love it, because I was alone . . . not that David hadn't been nice to me . . . and we were good friends, and I knew her well enough, and she thought she knew me well enough. And that's how I got over here.

It has worked out beautifully. We do not interfere with one another's affairs, but we go to many places together, and we have a lot of mutual friends. We've evolved the system now where we alternate getting dinner. She gets dinner for two people one night, and I get it the next night. And it's a very good system. In the first place, you live better when you cook for two people, and then you have one day free . . . you just don't have to think about cooking. We go out and eat a time or two, or we're invited out to friends, so it's really wonderful all the way around. . . .

I was 89 in November. I was born in St. Louis in 1889. My mother was one of the older ones of a large family, and we spent a great deal of time at her mother's house, which was not far from where we lived, so that I could always go there after school if my mother was out someplace. So I grew up around this family of older aunts and uncles. My grandfather was German and my grandmother was Pennsylvania Dutch. And on my father's side of the family, both grandparents were German from the old country. So in my early years I certainly was not brought up alone. In the evening we always had dinner together. My grandmother's long table was never taken down. All the young uncles could always bring friends home for dinner . . . but when you think of the work that went on!

My mother did quite a bit of the shopping, and she would take her younger brothers to buy their clothes and all that. So it all devolved on her, rather than my grandmother. I've always thought that my own mother was not too keen on big families, and I'm quite sure now that she just had enough of all the kids to look after. Of course, I did have an older sister, but she died very young, and I have no recollection of her at all.

I know I have cousins yet who talk about Aunt Carrie, my mother. She was the one they all turned to. If anyone got sick, she was the one that went for the doctor, because by that time, my father and I could do for ourselves. That was the kind of home relationship I had. There's not so much of that any more. Families scatter.

Well, I went through one grade school and one high school, all in St. Louis. And then I took kindergarten training school . . . that was before they opened up the College of Education. I took my practice training in public schools and got a job teaching kindergarten until I married. In those days, when you married, you were out of the school system.

Things are so different these days. I'm a feminist, shall we say, but I regret some of the things I think the "libbers" do. They don't do themselves any good. But I do think that the women's movement has been all to the good, because, first, the matter of salary for the same work. And I know, because I'm older and I've seen it. It took me longer to get an advance in salary, and status, on my job than if they'd had a man do it. I had to argue . . . not that they wouldn't advance women, because there were a number of women in good jobs, but it took longer to get there. But for the women to raise such a fuss the way it's been in the newspapers lately . . . I don't know. A mechanic on great big trucks! I think if a woman has some skills, she should employ them . . . I know it sounds old-fashioned . . . in a little more lady-like way. I don't think in this day and age that it's necessary for a woman to do that. But, if she's determined, why, that's her privilege, as far as I'm concerned.

Now, I've never felt put upon, but I do know around here that if you have a mechanic in to do some work or something, I feel just as sure as anything if there was a man telling the mechanic what he wanted done, it would be done cheaper and certainly faster and better. And I resent that. I feel the workman should not do that. It should be the job and not the fact that it's a woman who wants the job done. Vera had some electrical work done once or twice, and they just dawdled along. I said, "Vera, you should get real mad and cuss at 'em.". . . .

My mother lived to be 91, and she died of . . . well, just general disability. She had talked to the doctor who came to visit her periodically, and she talked to him and my husband

and me together before she died. She said, "I want to tell you now, because I know what I'm saying, but maybe the day will come when I won't. I do not want to be taken to the hospital and have all those tubes put in me just to keep me alive. I've lived a long life . . . longer than most people . . . and whenever the end comes, it's perfectly alright with me. But I do not want to be kept alive." And we agreed, because we felt that way too. I feel strongly on the subject, and my family knows it too.

My health is fine . . . oh, my rheumatic knees might be a little looser, but my doctor . . . I've had to change doctors a few times after they retired, you know . . . but my doctor told me only to come in if I have special problems. "Otherwise," he says, "next year we'll take more tests when you come in for your checkup. You're really in remarkable condition." I don't have high blood pressure. I watch my diet, and I have to restrain myself so that I don't put on too many pounds. Aside from that . . . well, as I say, my joints get stiff, but after I'm up and around, they loosen up.

I don't move as briskly as I used to do. For several years I had my little black poodle, and I took him for a walk every day, because he just lived for that. I used to love to work in my garden, but I can't do that any more, because I can't crawl around on my hands and knees. But I just love working with my houseplants these days.

I just hope and pray that I can keep moving and going right to the end. I tell the family, "If anything happens to me and I die suddenly, I don't want you to grieve about it. I want you to be glad that I didn't have to suffer." But I'm still amazed that I've lived this long. The time goes by, you know, and I don't feel anything but amazement. Here I am at this age, and I'm older than most people.

I've always had faith in religion. I've always done something around the church. As a girl, I sang in the choir for years and years. And then later, when I drove, I was the financial secretary of the church, even though I didn't handle any of the money. I went to church every Monday night for 11 years just to keep the records. It was a voluntary job, and you know what those are, but I found it very rewarding.

82 FIFTEEN PAST SEVENTY

I've always believed that if one door closes behind you, another door will open up in front of you, if you're just willing to sit for a minute or two and give it a chance to work, and not go off the deep end and carry on. It's not my way of doing things. I do believe that things work out right. Just be still, and let the events move. A lot of times you get yourself all worked up over something, and you fret and stew, and then all at once it resolves itself, and not the way you thought it was going to.

Things have gone up and down for me, but I haven't had the troubles the way some people have. My life at home when I was a girl was easy going, and my husband and I lived the same way. The one real trouble we had was during the Depression, but it didn't cause any family problems. We knew some people that had some really tragic results.

I believe that things will work out well. I don't say that I don't worry at all, but not much about me. I think that on the whole, most people make trouble for themselves. Of course, if you're blessed with good health . . . and that's one thing you're either blessed with or you're not . . . unless you really abuse yourself. Well, I've never been in a situation where I've really had to overdo. . . . With reasonable care, I'll be alright.

(Elna cancelled our first two appointments; she said her church and senior citizens and family activities didn't allow her the time to meet with me. I sensed that she was avoiding me. How wrong I was! When we did get together about five weeks after my first phone call, she could not have been more involved in the interview than she was. She was cheerful and relaxed, and she had been busy.

Enthusiasm stamps Elna's life. Throughout it she has been a mover . . . volunteering in church, supervising employees, gardening, investing her money, travelling . . . hardly the kind of person who is "willing to sit still for a minute and give it a chance," or content to "just be still and let the events move."

It sounded like a contradiction to me at first, but in reality there is none at all. The more I thought about Elna, the more I began to see the enthusiastic involvement and relaxed acceptance as simply different facets of an extremely "live wire" woman.)

11
There Always Are New Things to Discover

(My wife had seen Jeremiah Coulson *make a slide show presentation on the flora and fauna of Hawaii; she was delighted by the content of his lecture and the intensity of his conviction, and she suggested him as a candidate for an interview. He is 78 and an active conservationist. He lives in San Rafael, and, appropriately, redwood trees grow in the front of his house.)*

I don't know where all the time goes, but it does seem to go faster than it used to. There are so many stimuli these days, what with the radio and the television and all the stimulation that comes from the life we live. But if you live outside yourself, it's just natural to keep doing things. I do a number of interesting things. I do quite a bit of travelling, but not just for the sake of travelling or going somewhere. Life is very interesting for me.

I enjoy living as I do. In general, I have good health. Because of the association I have with the Academy of Science and the Alpine Federation and the Sierra Club and with some other explorations that appeal to me, there always are new things to discover . . . new campaigns to work for.

I guess I'm an organization man. I always inject myself into what's going on. I try to find out why things get done a certain way, and the next thing I know, I'm on a committee. I realized that the National Parks and wild areas and the environment would be lost or destroyed or diminished in some way unless there were people who not only enjoyed these things, but who were willing to devote themselves to efforts . . . meetings, speaking, writing, and whatever it takes to preserve them. I've been President of the Alpine Federation and I belong to the Sierra Club and the Audubon Society, and I'm active in the Academy of Sciences and a lot of other important conservation organizations.

I keep very busy. I've got so much reading to do that I could do nothing else but read all the time, but I don't want to do that. If I spend all of the time that I have just clearing out the house, I could do that too, but that's kind of working for a dead horse, you know. I want to live in the present and future most of the time, not in the past. . . . I make a lot of plans. I've got plans for the rest of the year, assuming I remain healthy. And I can think of things I want to do in the years to come. I do the things that have to be done. I make commitments.

I've been on the Docents Council of the Academy, and I've served on a number of special committees from time to time. It takes a lot of people to run the numerous activities, and I've done quite a lot of it at one time or another, not because I wanted to be in a position of authority, but I just thought when they asked me to help out, I ought to do my share. I do like docent work, because it brings me in contact with a lot of young people . . . and older ones too. I've made an appointment for later this month to do a Highlights of the Museum tour. But my specialty is the natural sciences.

I gave a show at the Academy not so long ago on three of the outer islands of Hawaii. I was on the first Sierra Club trip there in 1962, and I had taken a number of slides, so I was asked to put on this slide show. It took me a number of days to put it together. For almost 40 years, I've been taking color slides. An essential part of my life is photography. I don't claim to be a super-duper photographer, and I have to take an awful lot of pictures before I get one that I like, and in the course of time I believe that I've taken 100,000 slides. Of course, I've thrown out a lot too. So when I was asked to give that program on Hawaii, it took me quite a bit of time getting it ready.

I made a trip down the Salmon River in Idaho in 1949 with my brother, and the National Geographic Society got wind of it and asked me if I had any slides and would I write an article for them, which I did, and it was published. Later on they published a book on the U.S. National Parks and they used my material on Glacier National Park. . . .

Most of my friends are from either the Academy, the Sierra Club, or the Alpine Federation. After I retired, I decided to be a docent at the Academy and in the course of that, I've met some very fine people . . . and mostly women. I don't do much entertaining though. My brother comes and visits me once in awhile, but I don't have any parties here. I have a friend here in San Rafael who invites me over for dinner every once in awhile, and then when I reciprocate, I can either cook here or we can go out. I'm not limited to getting all my meals at home, but most of the time I do.

By living prudently, and with my house all paid for and with several sources of income . . . a pension from the company I worked for, Social Security, and a few modest investments . . . I can live comfortably. But I'm always looking for a way to save a penny or a dollar. I'm still driving a 12 year old car, and I take public transportation whenever I can. I don't want to get into a political controversy over Proposition 13, because it was good for some things and bad for others, but as far as I personally am concerned, it helped cut my taxes down.

I was brought up to be thrifty. Get your money's worth for everything. I don't always do it, but I try. I'm not a free spender on things, but if there's something I really want and I figure I can afford it, I buy it. Right now I'm seriously thinking about buying some cross country skis. I do a lot of skiing, but the downhill kind is getting to be a rat race, so I thought I'd like to try some of the other kind with a light weight ski.

I've been skiing for 40 . . . almost 50 years. Back in the 1930's we used to take standard width skis . . . the only kind available in those days . . . with a knapsack and go off touring through the woods and climbing the peaks. I did that for 20 years in different parts of the Sierra, and some outside of California too. I skied in Europe in 1961 and 1964, and I've skied in Japan a little bit too.

That's one of my favorite sports, but now I have spinal arthritis, which comes from living so long. Almost everybody has back problems of one kind or another. I have herniated discs so that I can't carry a heavy pack any more. But, as I told you, I'm thinking of getting a pair of lightweight cross country skis. I just make day trips on those and I don't carry a heavy pack at all.

One of the things that I do that I consider essential is a series of exercises every morning when I get up. I have a series of them . . . some were recommended by a doctor, some I got from the Canadian Air Force book, some are Yoga exercises suggested by a friend of mine, and others are ones I thought would be good for me. I do push-ups, jogging in place, and I work at it for 45 to 50 minutes every day. I do it quite religiously and I'm convinced that if I didn't do it, I'd become ossified. . . .

I was born in 1900 in Providence, Rhode Island. My father was a civil engineer, and my mother was a housewife. When I was about three years old, my father decided he wanted to break away from the New England tradition and seek his fortune in California. We lived in Mill Valley until about 1908, and by that time my father had bought the lot where this house is now. He designed the house and had some help in getting it built, but he lost a lot of money in a bank failure and so he couldn't finish it. But we at least had a roof over our heads until he could finish the job later on. So, outside of three or four years when my father took a job in Los Angeles, and the years I was going to college, I've lived here in this house ever since.

I had a happy childhood, although I'm sure that my father disciplined me. He used to have a strap and he whacked me on the behind sometimes if I did something that he thought was very bad. But, in general, it was a happy childhood, and I can't imagine that I had any traumas. There was one little incident . . . a happy one . . . that I thought of recently. As a child of five, when my brother was just a year old, I used to think it was funny to have this small baby kick me in the face, because his little feet were so soft. He was so small and his feet were so soft at that age . . . I don't know what made me think of that.

My father really liked the outdoors. When he first came to California he decided to look into the Sierra Club, and he went on walks with John Muir. From the very beginning, when I was a small boy, going on walks through the woods, and when my father was going on surveying trips and taking his little son with him, I got the chance to walk up around the hills of Mill Valley and Mt. Tamalpais. To me, it seemed just a natural development that I became interested in enjoying the beauties of nature.

I was very active in Boy Scouts here in San Rafael for a number of years, and I used to go camping with them. Later on, my brother and I went camping together. I've always been interested in the out of doors. And then I went on a camping trip with the Sierra Club in the first of what has become a very famous outing . . . the annual high trip . . . and that kind of triggered my interest in the club. When I got back home, I looked into it and joined. That was October, 1928, and I've been a member for 50 years. Through my association with the club, I came to realize that the beauties of nature will not remain unless there's some concerted action to save them. . . .

I never married. I came close to it a couple of times, but for one reason or another, I didn't. I'm a confirmed bachelor now, I guess. I think that's because of the obligation I felt for my mother. She lived to be 90 and I looked after her for a long time. There were times when I thought I could marry and take care of her too, and I was interested in a couple of women, but I decided that my obligation to my family was superior, so I didn't. But, who can tell? Maybe I'll find a companion yet. I don't have any set attitude toward it.

I manage to survive. I don't pretend to be a fancy cook. I don't go for highly seasoned foods, because some years ago I had a gall bladder removed. I find that highly seasoned foods disagree with me. I'm generally pretty much of a vegetarian

. . . not a confirmed one, but meat is expensive, and I like vegetables and rice and things like that. . . .

I retired from Pacific Gas and Electric Company as a staff engineer. It was administrative work. My training was in electrical engineering, but after I started working for them, I had a good deal to do with writing instructions and operating practices. In other words, I always had occasion to use the language. I like studying the English language. I'm not an expert at it, but as a result of that, I've become interested in studying foreign languages. I've travelled in Japan and I studied Japanese some, and I speak a certain amount of French. I've been studying Spanish for years. For several years I've been conducting tours in France, and I have another one coming up this July, and knowing the language is invaluable. Conducting a trip like mine involves not only the logistics of getting people from place to place, but also trying to make appointments for them to see some of the conservation problems in France, or in other countries that we visit. . . .

I mentioned living outside yourself earlier. Well, it's the opposite of living within yourself all the time. I live outside myself because I have contacts with people. I think that all my life I've made a point of trying to get along with people. That doesn't mean I always agree with them. Even in the Boy Scouts, there was this troop committeeman who was an uncle of one of the boys. . . . Well, he was kind hearted but autocratic. I remember my mother wondering how I could get along with him. But I could see what he was really driving at, and what some of the things were that stood in the way of our getting along together. So I made a point of getting along with him. And today, if I don't like somebody, I'd rather avoid having anything to do with them, unless I have to. And if I do, I can get along with them.

Living outside yourself is relating to other people. People who live within themselves are on the way to defeat. The natural thing in life is to relate to things outside . . . other people, beautiful scenery, interesting scientific things. And so long as you maintain an interest in them and not get distracted by your infirmities or ailments, then life is sort of open and expanding. But if you live within yourself, all kinds of things close in on you as you get older, and I think you're on your way to defeat.

I have, and I can get a great deal of satisfaction from going out someplace and watching some of the processes of nature going on. Some of them are very large, like watching a snowslide or seeing the tides come and go, and others are microscopic, like the flowers and the little tiny bugs that help pollinate them. I think that all of these things . . . enjoying the marvels and beauties of nature . . . take you outside of yourself.

But as you get older, the little infirmities come up. Your eyes don't see as good as they used to. Your hearing isn't as good. The joints don't work well, even though it's not the result of injury or trauma. There's a gradual deterioration of the body. I can't do as vigorous things as I used to do. In accepting it, you come to realize the inevitability of death.

There are times when you can't help think about death. I accept it as inevitable, but I don't fear it. I've been in a couple of situations when I thought I was close to it. One time, we were on a ski trip and we almost got frozen camping out in the snow without any camping gear. We were overtaken by a blizzard, and I didn't know whether I was going to get through or not. But I can't say I have much time to worry about it. Some people have premonitions or they worry about it, but I don't.

There are two factors that put me ahead of the game. Oh, there are a lot of others, but two outstanding ones. . . . One is genetic inheritance and the other is environment . . . in other words, how you take care of yourself. Well, I've done my best to take care of myself, although I've probably done some things that weren't too good. And I must believe that I have a certain amount of genetic inheritance. My father was 75 when he died. My mother lived to be almost 90, and my grandmother was 82, so our family was generally long-lived. My brother is 72, and he seems to be in good health too. All the indications are that he'll go on for quite awhile. So there are those two things . . . genetic inheritance and how you cope with your environment.

Some people, of course, no matter how they try to cope, the environment is too much for them. Miners that get black lung disease or asbestos poisoning . . . they live and work in some place where no matter what they do, there's something about the environment that's going to get 'em. But to the extent that we have some control over our environment . . . how we modulate it . . . I think that people can, if they want to go on living, do things that will help them.

I have a feeling . . . I can't give any specifics . . . that people who have done a lot of mountain climbing and sustain their interest in it generally live longer lives. I think that probably the exercise at higher altitudes helps them to develop their circulation and their lung capacity. And if they keep it up, I think it promotes longevity. And I'm sure that the discipline of taking one step after another toward your goal, and overcoming your frustrations as you go along, can be applied to any work you're doing. When you find that one route won't work, you have to take another. You learn that if you take things a little slower, you'll make better progress. There's usually no shortcuts for the hard work. In mountaineering, I've seen times when shortcuts have led to disaster. Many times, when I have been faced with some task or project that in itself was not related to the mountains, the thought of a mountaineer's persistent, steady pace has motivated me to continue. Patience and perseverance are key motivating factors that keep me going.

(*The precision on Jeremiah's desk . . . every pencil, piece of paper, notebook, file basket in exact alignment with each other . . . seemed to me to match the precision in his life. His description of himself as an organization man could not have been closer to the mark. I admire the way he has organized his life and followed his interests. I think there must be a relationship between his ordered approach to his activities and his ability, at age 78, to ski and lead trips to foreign countries.*)

12
Nobody Owes Me Tomorrow

*(Gloria Sherman is 80. She lives in an
exceptionally well-run home for the aged in
Berkeley. I avoided calling her for an
appointment for a long time after her name was
given to me because I was uneasy about visiting
an "old folks home.")*

I'm so glad to meet you. . . . Do you have any yarn? That's a
habit of mine that's been going on for 11 years, and everybody
I meet, I chisel. Right now, that looks like a big pile of yarn
over there, but actually it isn't and there isn't enough of any
one color. I could use more of everything except black or dark
blue or brown. That's because it's hard for me to see it at night
time, and I like bright colors anyway. Colors have an effect on
you. They give you a lift. If you dress in black all the time,
you're bound to feel morbid. I spend a lot of time knitting and
crocheting. And it's very interesting . . . while my hands are
busy, they don't shake, because I have Parkinson's disease.

It's a great help to me. It goes back a few years. When my
children flew the coop, and then later when my husband died,
I was left with a terrible emptiness. I felt I wasn't needed
anymore, and I have to be needed. So I looked around for
several months and then one day I went on a tour of a new
facility for multi-handicapped children run by the City of
Richmond. Halfway through, there was a little voice inside
me that said, "Gloria, this is it, if they'll have you." The
mothers of those children were fantastic. You know their

hearts were aching, but they referred to their children as God's chosen.

Anyway, I started making things for the children . . . afghans, bed slippers, bonnets . . . things like that. I worked there before I came to the Home here, and I'm still working for them right here in this room. No matter what it is, I want to help to the best of my ability. Maybe it's just to satisfy my own egoism . . . I don't know . . . but when I go up there . . . some friends in Richmond take me once in awhile . . . I come away with such a glow. I can't explain it . . . it's just that I feel privileged to know these women and that I've brought some happiness to some mother or child. I say, the good you do, you get back, and I get the love and the satisfaction from helping someone who's unfortunate.

I certainly got love back from my family. I've been very blessed. I've got seven grandchildren and five and seven-eighths great-grandchildren . . . the seven-eighths is on the way. I'm thankful the good Lord has spared me to see them. I had three children of my own. My son was a Lieutenant General in the Army. After he was in for 22 years, he had a heart attack and he went on a disability retirement. And then he developed cancer. And the day they develop a cure for cancer . . . I don't drink . . . but that day I'm going to get drunk. My oldest daughter lives in Monterey, and when she comes to see me, she has to drive 240 miles round trip, so I don't ask her when she's coming again. My second daughter, the middle child, lives in Albany, which is right near here.

I was married 49 years. If I had known what marriage was going to be like, I would have married sooner. I was 18 and he was 23. He was a pharmacist. I met him at a party given by a friend of mine. I couldn't see him at first, but my mother fell in love with him, and she used every trick she could think of to get us together. She was right. We had a wonderful marriage. The main thing was we liked each other, and we were friends. We enjoyed each other, and we had a good time raising the children. We were young ourselves, and we just grew up with them. I had three children in 29 months, so I was a busy lady. I wish I had that pep today. But they done me proud.

About a week after this old family picture here was taken, we had a traumatic experience. My oldest daughter got polio, and in those days they didn't hospitalize you so fast. So I sent the other children to my mother's, and my husband was the only other person allowed in or out of the house. Well, I had two clotheslines from the bedroom windows to the yard, and one day my husband came home from work and he asked me what the matter was. I said, "Oh, I'm so unhappy. I did the washing today, and I only filled up one line. I'll be so glad when they're both full. Then I'll know my family is well." Then when my children were all back home, my husband came home one day and he noticed that I was down in the dumps, and he asked me what the matter was. I told him I was so tired from all the washing, and he said, "Your family's well, isn't it?" And from then on, every time I hung out the wash, I used to say, "Thanks, God," because I knew my family was well.

I used to take my daughter to the Jewish Community Center swimming pool for her therapy. Well, they were going to have a swimming competition and she wanted to enter. My husband and I didn't know what the right decision was. If we don't let her do it, we're telling her you're not getting well. If we let her, and she can't do it, how will that affect her? Finally, we decided to let her do it . . . she's gotta find out for herself . . . and she came in third place! Our emotions . . . it's the first time that I saw my husband cry. . . . And she swims today . . . she loves to swim. . . .

Did you know that there were four generations of us born in San Francisco? On my mother's side, my grandfather and grandmother were pioneers . . . they came in 1850. He was a poor businessman and he lost every venture he went into. My father comes from Germany, and he and his three brothers came to the United States because they didn't want to serve under the Kaiser. They came to New York, but how did they get money, and how did they get to San Francisco? Oh, there were so many questions I should have asked him, but I never thought of it at the time. Anyway, he met my mother and they fell in love. He wanted her to name the day for the wedding, but she wouldn't until he got his American citizenship. And, by golly, he did. I thought it was kind of cute on my mother's part. She was 74 and my father was 71 or 72 when they died. I'm the only one that's gone beyond 75.

I was born in 1899, the turn of the century, in a house at 19th and Mission Street. I had two brothers. My older brother died when he was 20 months old. He was crawling around the kitchen and my mother had a pot of hot soup in her hands and she didn't see him and accidentally spilled the whole pot on him. Then I had a brother who was 17 months younger than me. Oh, he was gorgeous . . . he was my pride. He got hurt in a basketball game, and he died in his sleep a few days later. I went to wake him up to go to work, but he was already dead. It's taken me years . . . I never will get over it.

No, my childhood was not 100% happy. In the first place, I lived in district where I and about three others were the only Jews, and the kids used to taunt us. I remember this one horrible thing so well: "Red, white, and blue / Your daddy is a Jew / Your mother's a broomstick / And so are you." And I was called a Christ-killer. I'd go home and ask my mother if I killed Christ, because I didn't know what they were talking about. . . . And, all in all, my father was not a good provider. He was a tailor, and a good, kind man, but a provider, he wasn't. So my mother took in boarders and worked very, very hard. It was kind of hand-to-mouth . . . we never went hungry, but it was a hand-to-mouth existence.

I was always a poor student at school. Arithmetic was my terrible subject. When I graduated from grammar school and went into high school, my mother picked my subjects. There was something about the word algebra that she liked. "Oh, that's a beautiful sound," she would say. If her daughter took algebra, it would be like my-son-the-doctor, you know. So, among the courses was algebra, and every time I raised my hand to ask the teacher what the X stood for, she didn't answer me. I didn't know what in the world I was doing, so I quit school and went to business college. I became a stenographer, and I had several jobs which I loathed, because I couldn't stand the confinement of a one-girl office. So, I guess if you want to call me a dropout, that's what I was.

At one point when we had some financial reverses after I was married, I worked for two years in a dress shop. But other than that, I made a home for my family. I always considered myself a homemaker, not a housewife. To me, a housewife has always been someone you paid. . . . Occasionally, I would get a piano-playing assignment.

I had a natural gift for the piano. In fact, I used to play at Woolworth's on Market Street, selling sheet music before I was married. I loved that job because there were always lots of people around. And I learned three languages there, did you know that? I learned slang, profane, and English. But anyway, I can't play anymore.

A week ago Sunday, there was nobody on the floor here, and I thought I'd go into the solarium and see if I could practice a bit and play. I sat down and couldn't hit a chord with my left hand. As hard as I tried, I just didn't have the strength for it. I came back to my room and cried. But nobody ever sees my tears. It's my loss. I don't want anyone to cross the street when they see me coming, you know what I mean? I don't want sympathy. It's my tragedy. . . .

When my husband died, my children turned to me and said, "Mother, we've got a room for you." I said to them, and I've never regretted it, "Are we still friends?" They said yes, and I said, "Well, let's keep it that way." It's really much better that way, because there's a generation gap between me and my girls. And I can stay in this beautiful room and do as I please without the oh-mother-this or the oh-mother-that. They don't boss me maliciously, don't get me wrong, but they figure I'm behind the times.

A very dear friend and I were talking about this place one day, and she said . . . because she knew how frightened I was living alone . . . "Gloria, why don't you take a look at it?" So we did, and I spoke with the Social Worker here, but I still wasn't quite ready for it yet, so I told her to put my name on the list for the future. Then two years later, my physical condition was deteriorating so much that I just had to come.

Of course, it took a little pushing by our wonderful rabbi, but I've been here three years now, and I must say that in the home here there's a wonderful feeling of security. There's something lacking with the food, but it's an institution.

I had to sell out my belongings when I came here, and it made me feel so terrible that people were belittling the things that were so precious to me. When you come in to a place like this, you come with your clothes on your back . . . all your worldly possessions gone, and you're regimented. It's a traumatic experience to overcome. It's taken me quite awhile, and I've had to work on myself. The first three months, I just stayed in my rom, but then I said to myself one day that it had to stop. "You gotta make friends," I told myself. So I proceeded to make friends with the nurses, and, God Bless their hearts, they're just beautiful. One of them said to me, "You know, Gloria, you're the dirty old lady of the Home. We didn't laugh until you came here." I have a wonderful affiliation with the help here. I'm extremely fond of them, and they're extremely fond of me.

I made three rules for myself when I came in here. The first is I will not gossip. If people start gossiping, I just walk away. I just will not be a part of any intrigue. Then, I will not listen to the past or what might have been. You can't change it. I've had my joys and my sorrows and tribulations, but it's past and there's nothing I can do about them. And the third one is I will not listen to organ recitals. You know what I mean by an organ recital? . . . Your organs . . . your insides. Everybody has something wrong with them, and if you talk about it, you magnify it. I know what I've got and I know that I'm going to have to live with it, and that it'll eventually be fatal. But I want to laugh and joke every day that I can open my eyes. I'm just 80, and I figure that every day I opened my eyes, I'm living on profit. Three score and ten is 70, so I have a profit of ten years.

I say hello to everybody here. Some of the people I like better than others . . . that's only normal, but I will not slight anybody. Nobody's going to tell me who I can or can't be friends with. But I'm a little bit of a loner now. I shouldn't be that way, but I enjoy my television and my knitting and crocheting, and I'd rather be in my room.

I watch television a lot. I'm an addict. I like quiz games . . . challenges. I don't do any reading anymore, because I've had eye trouble. I had cataract surgery last year, and I'm still not adjusted to my lenses. I've got to be very careful, and I'm doing things I said I never thought I could do again. But don't ever say never, because you can do 'em. Nobody was going to show me the edge of the sidewalk or help me down the stairs . . . Oh no, not me! But I need help now and I ask.

Thank God for this knitting and crocheting. If I didn't have that, I'd be pretty bored. I get up every day at 7:30, go down for breakfast at 8:00. Lunch is at noon . . . that's the main meal . . . and then a light supper at five o'clock. They try very hard to have a different activity every day. They have different classes where you can speak up . . . poetry and that sort of thing. Right now, they're trying to work up a bridge group. They do everything in their power to make you comfortable and happy, but it's quite a problem, because they're bound to run out of things for you to do.

So many of the people here are verbally cruel. One day, two women even had a physical argument and one hit the other with her cane. Terrible! There's quite a bit of bitterness and jealousy. I think that's something that comes with being senile. And a lot of them criticize their children because they don't do enough for them. They're always listening to the past, which is one thing I will not do.

The average age here is 86, so I'm one of the youngsters. And I've got a boyfriend here. He's 97, and, oh, he's so sweet. I've known him for 30 years. It's been a delightful friendship, and he is the sweetest guy. He's got $5 and when he gets $10, he says we're going to Las Vegas and get married. It's all a laugh and joke. Of course, the women outnumber the men here. A few men have come in the last few weeks, but they're all senile. I should use the word confused rather than senile. And you just have to take it casually when somebody in the back wing that has been a vegetable for years has passed away. You just say to yourself, they're at peace. . . .

The money to keep me here is mostly from savings. I liquidated everything I had just before I came here. I had a few mutual funds, and I have Social Security and a veteran's pension . . . my husband was in the first World War, you know . . . I turn them both over to the Home, and the difference I have to pay. I came in with about $14,000, and I'm down to about $1,000. There have been two raises since I've been here. . . . $50 this year and $45 the year before. But I'm going to make application to MediCal . . . they allow you to have $1,500 of your own, so they'll pay the difference between what I pay. And then, no more worries.

Besides, what good does worry do? What's to be will be. Take it as it comes. I have to face my problems. Nobody owes me tomorrow. I just make the best of each day, because I know my years are numbered. My funeral is all paid for, because I don't want to be a burden to my girls even in death. So I don't worry about it. I've got three meals a day waiting for me, and there's security here . . . mentally and physically.

I have no real regrets. If there are any, they're all petty. In my experience, there's never a door that's closed to me, but automatically, not of my own choosing, another door is opened. That's the way I feel. I had some crises come to my life, and I got towards a decision, and I wondered . . . what do I do? . . . what do I do? But the door closes, and another one opens up, you know what I mean? It isn't that I made the door open . . . the opportunity just presented itself. It's like when I make a mistake in my knitting, and I get frustrated trying to correct it. So I just roll it up, put it aside, and the next day the solution comes to me. I don't brood over it. So I just face each day as it comes.

(Why, I asked myself, as I waited for the elevator after my interview with Gloria, had I been so apprehensive about visiting someone in an "old folks home?" Here is a lady whose hands tremble from Parkinson's disease knitting things she and others enjoy. She likes the staff, they like her, and she accepts the limitations of the institution she is in. Her sunny

sense of humor is contagious, and I had good feelings about the give and take of the interview.

The feelings plummeted as I walked through the main lobby. The chairs, empty when I had entered, were lined up along the walls, occupied by very old people who stared out the windows and hardly spoke with one another . . . mostly infirm, mostly women, and mostly barely ambulatory. There, in front of me, was the epitome of all that I had feared about my own old age.

My mind flashed back to Gloria, and I saw her in a new light. She was not only an oasis in a very barren desert, but hope for me, if I have to cross it some day.)

13

If Everyone Was Living Like I Was, It Would Be a Much Happier World

(Larry Wampler was dressed in a bright green sports jacket, in honor of St. Patrick's Day, he said, when we met in the lobby of the modern apartment building in downtown San Francisco. He is the father of a friend, 87, and living with a woman to whom he is not married.)

About 25 years ago I was down in Carmel, and Mrs. Scheuer was there on a two week vacation. I was there with a cousin of my wife . . . my wife had passed away in '54. We were married 37 years, and they were a wonderful 37 years, which may have something to do with the length of my life. Anyway, I met Mrs. Scheuer there and we've been together twenty-five-odd years, and we've gotten along very comfortably all during that time. It might sound unusual, but we've gotten along very well. If everyone was living like I was, it would be a much happier world.

It was my children who encouraged me to go to Carmel the weekend I met Pauline . . . Mrs. Scheuer . . . and by coincidence some of her children's friends and some of my children's friends were acquainted with each other. . . . We always tell the story of how I came down to a little lake in the back of the hotel, and how I got into a conversation with Mrs.

Scheuer. I was sitting on a bench near her and I apologized to her because I hadn't shaved, because I thought the noise of my electric razor might disturb the woman ... my cousin ... in the next room to mine. After I said that, Mrs. Scheuer detected that I wasn't married, and then I told her I had been a widower for about a year, and she told me she had been a widow for four years.

We started living together after one of the boat trips that our children suggested we make. We took separate cabins, and we got better acquainted with each other on the trip. We learned what our likes and dislikes were. Maybe if we hadn't taken those trips together, I'd be calling on someone else and having some other friend. But our relationship really started on that trip. And when we got back, I started visiting her at her apartment, and then we'd go out to supper, and it grew from that point.

Then we moved out to this retirement community in San Ramon to live, but we made it very emphatic that if there were any objections ... they're pretty high hat over there ... to Mr. Wampler and Mrs. Scheuer living together. ... Well, anyway, we never had the slightest trouble. We've never registered at any hotel as Mr. & Mrs. Wampler. We always go under our own names in case there's a phone call for either of us. I've tried to educate Mrs. Scheuer not to make apologies, which she sometimes does. But the circumstances have worked out better for us to operate this way without getting married.

The place in San Ramon was delightful, but it was too far from our children. Most of them live in and around San Francisco. So we decided to move into the city to be closer to them and for a little more excitement. I've lived here in this apartment for ten years and liked every minute of it. We've always had separate bedrooms for the twenty-odd years that we've been together, because we're more comfortable that way.

Frankly, it never occurred to me to get married again. We never have even talked about it. I mentioned it one time to my son, and he said it was up to me. So we've gotten along beautifully this way, and it's more advantageous financially not to be married.

Our tastes on things are not alike, but enough of them are to make us enjoy each other's companionship to a great extent. I think that contributes to the fact that we're in our 80's and, thank God, able to walk around and enjoy things and people. We love to meet strangers and find out where they come from. We made many trips, due to the encouragement of our children.

We've been to Mexico seven or eight times, and to Hawaii, of course. We've been to the North Woods of Wisconsin many times. We used to spend two months a year down in Carmel, and we've been on some very fine boat trips. We've been to several Central American countries, due maybe to my interest in stamp collecting. Pauline would like to go back to England, but I don't think I'd like to. It's too long a trip, and I don't think I could make it comfortably, so I wouldn't look forward to it. Her children have even tried to discourage us from going. But I don't think a year has passed where we haven't taken at least two trips.

We used to travel quite a bit by car, until about three years ago, I guess. We drove everywhere . . . Las Vegas, Florida, Wisconsin . . . and if I didn't take my car, we'd rent one when we got there. I still have my driver's license in my pocket. We don't travel so much anymore though. Right now we have reservations at a lovely hotel in Palo Alto. One of our grandchildren will drive us down. We'll have two rooms waiting for us there, and there's a little stream with fish in it. It's really beautiful, and it gets Pauline away from cooking and cleaning. And we take lovely walks in the surrounding area. It's very nice.

We don't have too many friends. The few married couples that we know are mostly gone. And when I left Chicago, I lost contact with the people that I knew there. We don't have too many friends, because . . . maybe it's because our children take up our time socially. I want to emphasize that one thing. I've got two great sons, and I really mean it. They're most attentive to me, and their children are too. Mrs.

Scheuer . . . Pauline . . . has had the same experience with her children.

An important thing in my mind is that we're able to take care of ourselves financially. We don't need our children's help and, as far as we know, they don't need ours, although it gives us pleasure to be of any assistance to the grandchildren when we can. But I think the situation where we don't feel we have to be supported by them is very gratifying. . . .

I went all through public schools in Chicago from kindergarten up. I went to La Salle High School, and I graduated from there in 1909, and that was the extent of my education and schooling. My father was a Dartmouth graduate, and I had made application to go there, but I realized I couldn't afford it, so I took a job instead and never went any further.

I was concerned with my father's drinking much of the time. I was concerned that we weren't getting to the top of the heap. We had a very nice home, but it was not too easy. My sisters . . . I had two very sweet sisters and a brother . . . and I got along well with them, but I was working pretty hard at different places at the time.

My mother died at 72 . . . I don't know what from . . . you can't call it old age at 72, can you? She was a Christian Scientist, for one thing, but I don't know whether that had anything to do with her death. My father died at 72 also, apparently in pretty good shape, but, as I say, he was a pretty good drinker, and I think that contributed to it. In my case, I don't drink and I don't smoke. I used to smoke cigars some years ago, but for the last 10 or 15 years, I haven't touched them. Before dinner I may have a little brandy, which is supposed to be good for me, but I can get along without it.

I would attribute the fact that I'm feeling pretty good at this stage of the game largely to luck. I've been very lucky. I've had several operations, and they've all been successful, but the more I've had, the less confidence I've had in doctors. The one I've got now though, is a fine man. He figures a little pain once in awhile, unless it's severe, isn't worth making all those fancy tests. The illnesses I've had, if you want to call them that . . . hernias and other things like that . . . have been properly treated, although some of them may not be necessary. But I've survived them, and I feel pretty good most of the time. As far as my faculties are concerned, I can hear and see pretty well, and I don't have arthritis like Pauline does. Oh, I had a little heart condition . . . a so-called heart attack, but I'm sure it was exaggerated. They put me in the hospital overnight . . . that was about five years ago . . . and that was that. I get just a little flair-up now and then, but it doesn't bother me. I think not worrying about yourself is one of the most important things of all. If it's going to happen, it's going to happen. I've lived a good many years, but if something happens in the meantime. . . .

When I die, as I've written to my children, my great hope is that I'll go to sleep some night and not wake up the next morning. I'd love very much to enjoy a few more years the way we're doing now, but I don't fear death. Oh, I may be a little more careful crossing the streets and obeying the rules to avoid accidents, but if there's any fear connected to it, it would be that I get a disease or get into an accident that would be a lengthy time before I die. I hope when something like that happens, it goes quick.

I don't worry too much. Sometimes I worry about my grandchildren getting along, but mostly I worry about little things. If you're supposed to be here at 10:30 and you're not here by 11:00, then I'll be wondering if something happened to you. Or, for instance, if Pauline says she's going to be back around three o'clock and it gets to be four, then I wonder whether she got across Geary Blvd. okay. Probably the reason for that is that we are very much on time for appointments, and I get concerned if other people are not. Little things, like a waiter not waiting while I make up my mind what to order, bothers me momentarily. I guess I'm just impatient. . . .

I met my wife when I was . . . let's see . . . when I was 24, and we were married in 1917. We probably went together about four years before I married, so I was about 19 or 20 when I met her. It was at a party given by a relative of hers. In those days, you went out with a chaperone. We used to take an elevated train ride out some place and buy ice cream cones, and so forth. And as my jobs got better, we went to dances and did a few things like that.

I had a variety of jobs. I can remember way back to the first one, cleaning the counters of a candy store, and then going into a sausage business through a friend of mine. And I went into a cooperage business, but the plant was a long way from Chicago, and I didn't enjoy it. I was very glad when my brother-in-law brought me in with him in a hotel and restaurant equipment house in Chicago. It was a very sizeable organization, and I stayed 15 years with them . . . very enjoyable. I eventually became sales manager for them. During that period, my father-in-law's novelty business was getting very prosperous, and he insisted I come in with him, because he had lost his only son. I was with him for a long time, but I didn't care for his life style. He was too much of a stepper for me, and he didn't get along with his wife, so I left him. After that, a good friend of mine persuaded me to come into the real estate business with him. And following that, another friend who was in the business of combining and buying out and selling businesses wanted to train me in that field, so I went with him. And that's the business I ended up in when I retired. I was his West Coast representative after I moved out here, and they still use my address, but it's a figurehead only.

It was a great shock to me when my wife died. She had a brain tumor, and she died in about two months. It knocked me cold for quite awhile. In fact, when I first came here, my doctor recommended that I see a psychiatrist, which I did for three or four times, because I was so depressed over the loss of my wife. It was such a wonderful marriage.

After she died, my boys moved out to California, and I wanted to get out there to be near them, so I came out on a visit in 1954 and I liked it, so I moved here. I got an apartment at the Press Club, even though I didn't have a thing to do with journalism. It was a 100% men's club at that time, and it didn't take me very long to like the fellows there. I was very active in the Club. As a matter of fact, while I was living there, I was going with Pauline . . . that was before we moved over to San Ramon together.

What pulled me out of the depression I was in was activity at the Club, and then, not long after that, meeting Pauline, and also just making up my mind that I was going to stick to my stamp hobby, and just realize that I had had a wonderful 37 years. And saying my prayers every night. I'm still probably the only one in my family that says their prayers every night.

Religion has never meant that much to me though. My mother was a Christian Scientist, but my father was never religious in any way. There was very little religion displayed in my family. I attended Christian Science services once in awhile out of courtesy to my mother more than for a belief in it. I don't like to say it, but I never considered myself a Jew, except that my grandparents were Jews, so I suppose that makes me one. But I don't attend Temple and never did . . . I think that a universal religion with everybody being honest and having faith that there's a Lord or something behind us all that keeps us going, suits me fine. Why He appeared to some people and not to others, I'm not going to bother about. . . .

I get up at 5:30 every morning and read the newspaper. I get almost through in an hour and a half. It takes so much time because the paper is getting thicker and thicker. But I enjoy the columns immensely. Then I go through some exercises some of the times . . . not as often as I should . . . and I shower, and about that time Pauline is through with her toiletry. Then we get out and walk on Polk Street for a couple of miles. We enjoy watching the people doing their shopping. We like to wander around there. Sometimes we go downtown on the bus, which only takes a few minutes. We come home before it gets dark, or whenever we're tired. And we go out to eat two or three times a week. Other times, Pauline cooks . . . simply. And we have our children over every week or so, or somebody in the building here that we're close to.

I have a hobby, but it's something I've neglected terribly. It's a division of stamp collecting called covers. Covers are the envelopes with the stamps on, designating that they're different, in that they're addressed to different people, and there's no two alike. I hope soon to get back to it. Once in awhile I dabble in it, and I've got a pretty good collection, which I'm giving to the boys, so that the ownership will follow me. Sometimes I do it in my spare time . . . like when Pauline goes to a luncheon or whatever it is. During my years at the Club, I used to spend at least a couple of hours every day at it.

In the evenings we enjoy our Telefunken radio very much, because we turn off a lot of the dumpy programs on television. We happen to be old fashioned enough to enjoy Lawrence Welk, and we listen to the news, of course. I like Washington Week in Review and Wall Street Journal. And, of course, if there's a ball game on, I'll watch that.

I like to see cheerful shows. Comedians interest me a great deal. As far as sports are concerned, I'm a great baseball fan. I've always loved baseball. That's the only thing that Pauline and I don't get along too well on. Oh, I don't mean not get along . . . it's just that our ideas are entirely different. She's a lover of symphony, and I'm not. But we don't argue. We have two televisions, so it doesn't matter too much. She tries to watch some of the games, but it's been a pretty hard job for me to educate her as far as the strategies are concerned. But baseball and football interest me considerably. I never was much of an athlete; I was just a good attender. My father used to take me to see the Chicago White Sox. We'd sit in the bleachers for 15¢ and we enjoyed it. But now, it's become very commercial and it doesn't worry me too much when the Giants lose. . . .It sounds ridiculous, but I don't seem to have the time to sit down and read a novel. . . .

Pauline tells me I have a sense of humor, and I realize that I must have one, but I don't know what I can attribute it to. Could it be possible that it comes from my sons? Both of them have good senses of humor. We have a secret language between us at times. We understand each other's jokes, but no one else does. It's been a lot of fun for me. . . .

I don't think I'd do things much differently. Perhaps I might have pursued a connection with the founder of Sears Roebuch, and I probably could have gotten further along in business, or I might have gone into different vocations, and I probably could have made more money, but what good would that have done me? There's a song that we used to sing at the Press Club called "If I had my life to live over, I'd live over the corner saloon."

("Could it be possible," Larry asked me, with a twinkle and a grin, "that [my sense of humor] comes from my sons?" I don't doubt that they have a good time playing straight men for each other, but what Larry certainly does get from his sons . . . and from Pauline . . . is a lot of nurturing love. The love must have something to do with his sunny disposition. Whenever I think of him, the title of a Broadway musical comedy of a few years ago . . . A Most Happy Fella *. . . comes to mind.*

Larry is a talker; he's the kind of person an interviewer appreciates. But he is also a listener. Of all the people whom I interviewed, he was the one who most quickly and fully understood why and for whom I was writing FIFTEEN PAST SEVENTY. *I appreciate him.)*

14

I Always Try to Look at the Bright Side

(Pauline Scheuer *has deep blue eyes and a handshake stronger than most men half her age. She is 85 and lives with* Larry Wampler.)

I like to get along with people . . . to be interested in their activities. If they tell you something you never heard of, I like to ask them, "What is it? What is it all about?" I would describe myself as a person who gets along very well with people . . . at least I try to get along with them. And if there are people who don't like me, too bad! But the main thing is to get along with Larry. And we do get along very well. He's really an awfully nice guy, and we have such a happy life. I'm very grateful . . . very lucky.

Do you know how I met Larry? Well, one time I had a two week vacation coming. My children said to me, "Why don't you go down South where you'll have warm weather and sunshine?" But I said I would be too lonesome there. I like to be close to here so they can visit me. So I went to Carmel, and my children came to visit me off and on. And one day, I was sitting at the pool, and a gentleman was sitting next to me. And I swear to you I never talked to any man, although I had been a widow for many years. And this gentleman said to me, "Would you excuse me please? I am not shaved this morning, because my lady friend" . . . he was staying there with his cousin . . . "because my bedroom is next to my lady friend's, and I was afraid if I would shave that my electric razor would make a lot of noise and disturb her." So I knew he wasn't married.

We talked and we talked, and then I said something which I never said before . . . never. I said, "When you get back to San Francisco, will you call me sometime?" And he called me and he took me out to dinner. After that, we made many trips together. We were in Mexico six times, and we were up in the woods of Wisconsin . . . and in Florida. And boat trips . . . once to Panama, and to Hawaii too. We always had such a good time together, and we met such nice people. It's lucky that we met.

What makes me especially happy is that my children are so very fond of Larry, and I'm not saying it just because he's sitting here. They are very fond of him. You know, they lost their own father when they were very young, and to them, he's just like their father. I never talk to my son that he doesn't say, "Let me talk to Larry." And they often go away with us on trips, and we have lovely times together.

But you know why I never got married to Larry? I'm getting a widow's pension from Germany. I get it once a year through the International Bank. I have to go to the German Consulate once a year and they have to verify that I'm not married yet. I would lose it if I were married.

None of my friends said anything at all when I moved in with Larry . . . at least they didn't tell me. But then, I don't have any friends who live together with a man. And my children are very much for it, and they really like him, and I think his children like me, which makes it nice. I mean, I could be a very nice person, but for some reason his children wouldn't like me. That happens. . . .

I was born in Freiburg in Western Germany, but my parents moved to Hanover soon after I was born, and that's where we lived. My father was in the textile business, and he was a typical northern German, you know . . . very authoritarian. I wasn't too happy with him, and I don't think my mother was too happy with him either. I don't know whether it's my imagination, but I have the feeling that my mother had a boyfriend, and I can't blame her, because of my father's attitude. She was very beautiful . . . exceptionally beautiful. But they stayed married all the time . . . until they were deported. . . . I was the only child.

It was very strange the way I met my husband. I had some friends that had a restaurant, and I was going inside to see them, and a man was going outside, and he kind of looked at me. And my friends that owned the restaurant told me later that the gentleman's name was Johann Seemann, and he had asked them who I was and whether he could meet me sometime. I remember that he came to my house and asked my mother whether he could take a walk with me. And I had to have sort of a chaperone with me. I wasn't allowed to walk alone with him. Anyway, we were married, and three or four years later my children were born. I have one son and one daughter.

I was about 22 years old when we were married, and we were living in Hanover. We had a very nice apartment there, and in Germany, in those days, you know, you had to have a cook and a girl who takes care of the children. And to this day, you know, I still, after all these years, get a birthday letter from her. . . . We lived in Hanover until Hitler came to power . . . that was in 1933 . . . and I kept begging my husband . . . I can see myself begging him on my knees next to his chair, "Let's leave. Let's leave." But he didn't believe that Hitler would last, you know? But then, one day, I remember my son came home from school, crying his heart out. He was 16. I said, "What's the matter?" And he said, "I had to write something on the blackboard, and the boy who came after me wouldn't touch the chalk because I'm Jewish. I'm the Jew that touched the chalk."

That was very strange, you know, because religion was not at all . . . not even a little bit . . . important when I was a girl in my family. You know, in Germany, we didn't have religious classes. We had to go to separate religious classes, and I remember my parents were sending me to some Jewish school, but I didn't go very long . . . maybe two times, and not again.

Anyway, after that . . . that was in 1939 . . . my husband

listened to me, and we left for England, hoping we could get to the United States. We stayed in London with very, very lovely cousins. We thought we would stay there for maybe a week or two, until we could get our visas, but it took a year and a half. We were not the only ones who stayed with my cousins. She accommodated six or seven families, sleeping on the floor of her kitchen . . . dining room . . . everywhere.

When we got to the United States, we came to San Francisco, and then my husband started to work for a very short time for . . . I have such a bad memory . . . for Levi Strauss. But then he took sick. He had a heart attack. In those days . . . I never forget that . . . they put you in bed for such a long time. He was in bed for five solid years. That was in '45, and he died in 1950. . . . I had a good relationship with my husband, but not so happy as with Larry. He was a little like my father . . . dominating. But the sad thing was that he was sick for so many years.

When we left Germany, my father and my mother were still at home. When we came here, I said to my husband that one of these years we were going to bring them along to America, because, at that time, we didn't have enough money, and they were old people, and we would have to support them. But in that period, they were deported to Auschwitz and killed there.

When my husband died, I had to go to work, and that was the first time I had to do that, except that while he was sick I was even then sewing gloves at home to bring in a few dollars. So then, I started to work for little store that sold jewelry and watches. I never forget . . . I went there . . . somebody had told me that the man was looking for someone to work there. When I came there, he talked to me, and he said, "I'm going to think about it and I will let you know." I had the feeling that was the end of it, so I said to him, "Why don't you try me for a week or two? If I don't work out, you'll let me know." Well, I was with him for 12 years, so he must have been satisfied with me, don't you think?

After that, I worked for a ladies wear store. I never forget . . . the girls there had been working for that man for 20 or 30 years, and I was new, you know. They were so jealous of me because, first, I was new and younger than they were, and, secondly, strangely enough, ladies would come in and ask for a dress, and they would always ask *me* to show it to them. . . .

I have no special hobbies . . . except for my interest in music. I've always loved music. As a child, I had piano lessons, and I played a little, but not too well. I think I must have had singing lessons, because . . . you see, after my husband's death, I started going to symphonies again. . . . Anyway, shortly after that I started singing with the symphony here in San Francisco. That was about 20 years ago, I think, and they checked me out first, you know? I had to go there for a try-out, and I can still see my children and three of my grandsons sitting there in the audience. So I sang in the chorus, and I did that until I met Larry. I would still go to the symphony, but I don't like to go alone when it gets dark.

I don't read much any more, because I have a little trouble with my eyes. I went to have them checked, because I was told I had a tendency to cataracts. So now Larry reads to me. And we watch television. I like the lighter things . . . All in the Family . . . Love Boat . . . and we both watch Washington Week in Review. . . .

I never have any fear of dying. I mean, I would be afraid if I would be sick for years and years, knowing that it would lead to death. But fortunately, both of us are in pretty good shape. Oh, I have arthritis that hurts pretty bad, even when I'm lying in bed, but it wouldn't kill me. I try not to worry about the future. Why should I worry whether I get sick or Larry gets sick or something like that. I mean, I look forward to the future, but to the near future . . . like I'm looking forward to going to Palo Alto at the end of the month with Larry. But otherwise, I don't try to worry. I always try to look at the bright side.

(Larry introduced me to Pauline when I came to interview him. She asked to be excused when I turned on the tape recorder, but she never left the room. She stayed on and listened to his responses. A little while later, she was prompt-

ing him when there was a detail she felt ought to be included. Still later, I was gently cautioning her that I was interested in his comments, and that I'd get hers on tape at some other time. Almost without realizing it, I had found another person to interview.

I had the same mock battle with Larry while I was interviewing Pauline. I was almost rude to him, pretending I hadn't heard his prompting and explaining. But Pauline comes through in her own dignified, soft-spoken way. She is a giving and caring woman. In turn, she is nourished by the caring she receives from Larry and all of their children. I believe it is the mutual caring that contributes to her vitality. The vitality certainly shines through her deep blue eyes.)

15
My Practice Is a Joy to Me

(With the sole exception of Leonard Watanabe, I had not known any of the people I interviewed. I have seen him once every six months or so for the past 20 years, but only in a dentist-patient relationship. During that time, he seems not to have aged at all. He is 85 and still practicing full time.)

I've been pretty lucky with my health. Naturally some times I don't feel so well, but then I dress up and go to the office and I feel a lot better. You know, a lot of patients come in with a cold and you feel that you may have caught one from them, and, psychologically, it makes you feel kinda bad. But I think that if it's not a serious illness, it's better to be up and around.

One thing I've learned about staying healthy . . . you see, when I was in high school, I ran long distance. The coach used to say, "In training, run twelve long blocks or fifteen short blocks, but when you come to the last block, be able to sprint fast . . . real fast. If you can't do that, you're not running to your capacity. If you're all exhausted at the last block, you'll never win. So gauge your strength and train yourself so that you have enough power for the last block."

Well, I think, interpreting that . . . if you don't exert yourself to the point of straining, then you're doing yourself more harm than good. So, know your capacity . . . know what you can do, and keep that up. That's what I do in my routine. I get up at a certain hour and go over to the office and do the amount of work that I'm capable of, and I don't get tired or exhausted by the end of the day. I have plenty of energy, not like some of these fellows who are so exhausted at the end of the day that they go home and have supper and that's the end. I don't feel that way.

I don't do as much physically as I should, except that over at the office I try to walk as much as I can. I don't send the girl over to the laboratory . . . I make it a point to go there myself, and that's about a half block, you know, and I don't know how many blocks I walk a day. That's my exercise. I really ought to do more. I feel as though I'm not getting around. My arms are getting smaller, I notice, and with the type of work I do, I don't use enough muscle. But I don't have any tremors at all. When you have tremors, of course, or when your eyes go bad, you can't practice dentistry.

But I'm at the stage where I don't have to work any more. My kids are all educated and they're all in good health. I'm all by myself . . . and it's lonesome some times. The bad thing is my wife being gone. I don't know why the good Lord took her away. She died in an automobile accident about six or seven years ago. It was so tragic. She was very active, you know. She did a lot of work for the church . . . a lot of work for the women folks that used to come from Japan. You see, she was born in this country, but her parents were Japanese, and she spoke both languages. In the older days, when people came from Japan, they didn't know where to go to find an American doctor, and they didn't know how to tell him what they wanted. So my wife used to take them and help in so many ways. She has so many good friends. . . .

I don't have too many friends any more. It seems like most of my contemporaries are going. When you say friends, you know . . . friends that you've had 15, 20, 25, 30 years . . . that kind of friend is getting less. But I've got all kinds of acquaintances in some of the organizations I belong to. I belong to the Japan Society and the Japanese-American Citizens League, the Chamber of Commerce, the Osaka-San Francisco Sister City Committee . . . anything that's related internationally or that has as a basis or aim to promote better feelings between the two countries. I've been on the Board of

Directors of Osaka National Bank for a good many years. I didn't know anything about banking, but they wanted me in because I had been in busines a long time and I had Japanese patients. So I went in with them. Anything that has to do with Japanese-American relations I seem to get pulled into. So I have a few friends from years ago and a lot of acquaintances that I make by going to meetings. . . .

I usually get up around six in the morning and have my breakfast at home, and then I start for the office around seven. It takes me about 40 minutes to drive to the office. I try to be there at least by twenty minutes to eight. That gives me sufficient time to get things ready on time, so that I can start in at eight o'clock. I've done that for years . . . ever since I started to practice, I guess. I like to start early in the morning, and I keep going till half past five, and I don't get out of the office till six or six-fifteen. By that time, the traffic isn't so bad.

My lunch usually is about 12, but sometimes I get a little delayed and don't get it then. On busy days, I like to have my lunch brought in so I don't waste time going out. Sometimes I take a long lunch hour, like today, I went to the Japan Society annual meeting. But I guess I put in about nine hours a day . . . except for Wednesday afternoons. But I come in on Saturday mornings all the time. I sometimes get a little break in the afternoon, but I prefer to keep on going. I'd rather not take too long a rest period during the day when I'm working. I like to keep going from one patient to another. So, usually my appointments are all taken up from eight o'clock on. And then, on top of that, I have emergencies. So I'm usually working straight through. I like it and the time goes very fast. You're right in gear, so to speak, and I find it very interesting that way. And I don't feel fatigued or tired at the end of the day.

When I come home, I keep myself doing something . . . like cooking. I can't make anything fancy, but I make something that I like. And then I've got all these books around here. Sometimes I pick up a journal or a magazine. I never run out of magazines. Last night I was looking at Smithsonean and National Geographic. Then I've got a good television . . . a Sony, and if there's a special program I want to watch, I see that. I like Masterpiece Theatre and the English plays . . . they're very good, and I like them very much. And I watch 60 Minutes on Sunday evenings.

Usually I go to bed around 10. That's my routine, you know. I guess if there's one thing I do, it's that. I wake up at a certain time and I go to bed at a certain time. And I think that the wear and tear on your system is reduced to a minimum. You can't be running around at night when you're practicing, and then get up early. I don't think you can keep that up too long.

I usually do my shopping on Sundays. I used to go to the Community Church when my wife was with me, but when she died, then my schedule changed around. I didn't know what to do and it was very difficult to get into the routine that I'm in now. It took me quite a long time to get adjusted. We had always gone to church from 11 o'clock on, but I've been kind of negligent about attending since she died. I like to hear a religious program that comes on television at 7:30 in the morning, so I don't feel I'm entirely a heathen.

My parents both felt that religion and education were very important. My father was a Buddhist minister and my mother was a Christian, and we always went to Sunday school and put on our Sunday-school-best clothes. Religion played a fairly routine part in our family. And when I got married, my wife's folks were very religious too. After we got married, we selected our church and the Community Church appealed to us and we liked the sermons there. . . .

I was born January 28, 1894 in the home of a plantation owner near Hanalei, Kauai. When my father and mother came from Japan, they didn't want to go to work in the fields. They sought some kind of work that would teach them about the American way of life. The planter's wife understood that and offered him a job as a cook, even though he didn't know how to do cooking. But he said he was willing to learn. And my mother was the upstairs girl who took care of the house.

But my father had always wanted to be in some kind of business for himself, so he saved up his money and started an import business in Chinatown in Honolulu. Well, the bubonic plague started in after awhile, and the government quarantined the whole area, and later they set fire to the whole area, so my father had to start all over again. Of course, the government compensated him pretty well, but he had to start all over again. And then we came to San Francisco in 1905. . . .

My folks used to take me to a Japanese dentist in Japantown here in San Francisco, and for some reason that I don't know, he kept telling my mother every time she went there to have all the kids' teeth fixed, "Oh, that boy has the talent to be a good dentist." And my mother got the notion from him that I should be one. She tweaked me constantly to go into dentistry. I didn't know what I wanted to do, but in those days, we followed our parents' wishes pretty closely. What they said was the law of the family. And, you know, it's a funny thing, three of my brothers were dentists too. I suppose my folks thought I was doing pretty well, so why not follow up something that's good. My youngest brother, Richard, went into mechanical engineering, and he's back in Hawaii, and he's doing very well for himself too.

I went to dental school at Cal in San Francisco and got out in 1917. My folks couldn't afford to start an office for me after they put me through college. But my father had a lot of friends, and they got together and put up $25 apiece. They got around $2,000 for me. I still needed another $1,000 so I got a loan from the bank and started in practicing in Japantown.

I realized pretty early in my practice that it wasn't a very good idea to confine myself to the Japanese trade only. I felt that in order to have a larger practice, you had to go out to the American public, but in those days it was practically unthinkable, because the anti-Japanese feeling was very bad, and the only avenue from which you could get your patients was the Japanese. So I had to stay where I was for the time being.

Around the time my younger brother graduated from dental school, I began to realize that orthodontics was practically unheard of among the Japanese, and that there were no Japanese orthodontists. I felt I wanted that kind of training, so I turned over my practice to him and went to Johns Hopkins University and finished my post-graduate work in orthodontics in a year. After that, I worked for two years as an instructor with the top man in orthodontics in Baltimore.

While I was back there, I made a trip here and I got married. It's a funny thing . . . my wife lived in the house next door to this house . . . that was long before I lived here, of course. I had some very good friends that knew her folks, and they used to go over to their house for a good Japanese dinner. One time they invited me, and that's how I met her.

I brought her back to Baltimore, but she didn't like it at all. You see, I had a pretty good offer there, and everything looked pretty bright to me. And another thing was I didn't like the way the Japanese were being treated in California, and I didn't want to raise my family in a climate of that kind. I wanted to make my roots in the East, where I was welcome. But she wanted me to come back. She didn't think it was the right thing for me, being of the second generation, to run away from this area. She had some good arguments, and she convinced me that I ought to come back to California and see what I could do in spite of all the anti feelings that were still going pretty strong. So I finished up my contract and came back and started up my practice again. She had a very hard time trying to find a place that would rent to Japanese, but she finally did. And then, two years later, this house was up for sale, and we bought it, and she was right back next door to where she was raised. . . .

I wanted to specialize in orthodontics because that's what I was trained in, but, as I said, among Japanese, orthodontists was practically unheard of. It was practically impossible to get any kind of patients among them. So, even though I wasn't quite ready to move downtown, I decided to do it anyway and try to break into the American public, even if it meant going into general practice. And that's what I did. That was about 1925, and I've been here ever since.

Around the time of the China War, when the Japanese were in Manchuria I had to take over my father-in-law's business when he got sick. He had a very big import business going . . . he was the one who introduced kimonos into this country . . . and my wife's family kept pressuring me to take over the business. So I kept my practice going on the weekends, and I worked the business during the week. I didn't know what I was stepping into, because it was a very difficult time to sell any Japanese merchandise. And every day, instead of getting better, things were getting worse.

When Pearl Harbor took place, that was the end. By golly, when I went to the store that next morning, there were soldiers at the door, and you couldn't do any business at all. I commuted every day, trying to liquidate the business, and every time I went through the toll gate at the bridge, they'd take me over to a place to get searched. They feared something like Pearl Harbor or that I was going to break up the bridge. Anyway, we finally got a permit to evacuate to Dallas . . . my family, my wife's family and my brother, Hiroshi.

We went to a hotel in Dallas while we were waiting for our furniture to arrive, and the doggoned detectives there came every day and pulled us into the station. We were put in with robbers and the other prisoners from morning to late afternoon every day. Then later, once a week. After we got settled in our house, about half a dozen men would come over in a machine, and, oh, they gave us a hard time. The neighbors were wondering what was happening, and it was so embarrassing.

After the war we came back here, and it was a little rough getting set up in my practice again . . . getting credit, when the feelings against the Japanese was still running so strong . . . but things have gone pretty well since then.

I have absolutely no plans to retire. I don't want to. I want to keep on going. In the beginning it was so hard, and I always felt that a Japanese dentist would have a hard time getting the feel of how to practice among the Americans. So, since I was the first Japanese dentist to go downtown, I felt that I should open my office for some of the younger people to kind of train them. I gave them the chance to practice without any kind of commitment or contract. They could stay as long as they wanted to, until they got enough experience and money to go out on their own. There were about 15 young dentists who came through my office. . . .

I found that if you keep on going and keep it up regularly, it becomes a routine . . . with a minimum of stress. I think that's the whole thing . . . less stress. In the early days of my practice, I used to worry like anything, because you don't know exactly what to do. You have the training to do things in a certain way, but it doesn't always come out exactly like that. Each individual is different. When you come up against something unusual, then you're up against it, and you worry and you think and you do a lot of reading and things like that. But gradually, that type of extreme stress is not so prevalent like it used to be for me. So, my practice is a joy to me each day now.

You meet people that you like. There's no friction of any kind. You're not fighting. You're not competing. You're not trying to find out how to beat somebody else. This way, it's easier. People have a trust in you, and if you're honest with them, they're honest with you. It makes life worthwhile.

The secret of success in my practice, which is something I derive a great deal of joy from . . . you're not just a patient and doctor. It's a little bit more. There's a kind of friendship feeling between the patient and you. I've had children for patients that come back to me with their children. I have many third generation patients. So, it's meeting old friends constantly.

(*As much as anyone can enjoy going to a dentist's office, I have always enjoyed my visits to Leonard Watanabe's. He is always cheerful and sensitive to the pain in my teeth as well as the drain on my check book.*

He is a remarkable man . . . remarkable for his commitment to his practice and his patients, for his vigor, for his ability to surmount the horrendous obstacles to his career, and for his cheerful, philosophical attitude, despite the obstacles.

When I have daydreamed about the kind of life I'd like to be leading when I get to be 75 or 80, words like skilled, productive, energetic, cheerful, and sensitive have continually popped up. After having interviewed Leonard, I have a real life model to focus on. The only thing I'd want different for my life is to have my wife with me.)

Epilogue

Interviewing the 15 people in this book was an extraordinary voyage. When I began, I wanted to know how they are different from the "loners" and "losers," and what they need to be able to enjoy their old age. When I finished, I found more comfort in my present age and less fear of my old age. Along the way, I had frustrations and doubts ... would I ever find the answers I was looking for? ... would I ever lose my fear of growing old? ... would I ever have the spare time again to watch the Monday night football game on TV? ... but they were nothing compared to the rewards that came from talking with the Fifteen. There were delicious little moments, like hearing Taylor Patterson say, "Hi, Jim!" when I telephoned him several weeks after our interview, instead of the "Jim who?" before. There were insights that left me feeling so light that I was sure I could fly. The discovery that death, for me, was a sad, not a frightening, event was one of them.

To get to that point, I had to give up a lot of hunches and ideas about what it takes to enjoy old age ... preconceptions around which I had framed questions about health, diet, physical exercise, relationships with the opposite sex, money, religious faith, childhood experiences, social involvement, and long-lived parents. Actually, they weren't that hard to give up; the answers I was given simply refuted them.

I have always believed, for example, that you must at least have good health and a modest income to lead a comfortable old age. Because I believed that, I faithfully adhered to doctors' prescribed back exercises and low carbohydrate diet, and I squirreled extra dollars into my bank to insure that I'd be healthy enough and have money enough to enjoy my retirement years. And then I met Liz Farrell.

Liz lives on $312 a month in an attractive studio apartment, gets occasional financial help from relatives, and is proud that she had been able to put aside almost $600 into her savings account. She has survived a badly diseased spleen and an auto accident that fractured three vertebrae. Her abdomen is distended, and she suffers, from what my neighbor tells me, extremely painful bouts with arthritis. Liz has the lowest income and, by my standards, the poorest health of any of the Fifteen, yet she says she is healthy and financially comfortable. After talking with her, I'm no longer as worried as I used to be about what my life would be like without good health and a comfortable reserve in the bank, and I'm beginning to question their importance.

I felt sure that there's a clear relationship between a person's longevity and the life span of his parents, and that if his parents both died young of natural causes, his chances of living to a good old age were slim. But Elaine Wirth has lived more than 30 years longer than either of her parents, and I now wonder whether attitude isn't as important as genes.

I was always convinced that you can't expect to lead a satisfying old age if your young and middle years are unsatisfying. But I contrasted what Sheldon Greenwald told me about his first 58 years, which were miserable enough for him to consider suicide, with what he had to say about the next 27 happy years, and I'm not quite so convinced any more.

It just isn't possible, I thought, to be able to enjoy your old age if you live by yourself in a tired old apartment building, don't have friends, and can't read very well . . . in other words, if you aren't socially involved. But here was William Eckhardt playing cards at the Senior Center, cooking for his family, doing needlepoint for strangers . . . and enjoying himself! Social involvement, as I had defined it, is one more "absolute necessity" that I discarded.

One by one, all the other beliefs had to be discarded too,

and I was left without questions to ask or panaceas to look for. And then, without the questions to lean on for support, it slowly dawned on me that there is no one answer to enjoying old age, any more than there is to enjoying youth. It's a problem everyone has to solve for himself. I knew that "my" Fifteen were special people . . .that's why I chose them for the interviews . . . but they too had to find what they needed to enjoy the kind of life they wanted.

I also discovered that every one of the Fifteen looks forward to something in his life . . . Larry and Pauline to their trip to Palo Alto, Leonard to the next day at his office, Bud to his poetry, Elaine to Seniors for Quality Education. What they look forward to isn't important; it's the looking-forward itself that is. I found that discovery reassuring, because I see myself as a guy who's continually looking forward to the next project, and it's comforting to know that I share a common trait with those special people.

I look back at those awakenings and I wonder how I could have been so unaware and spent so much time looking for a simple, single answer. I should have known better. But that's O.K. I now recognize that the questions weren't as important as the questioning. The questioning was my way of moving toward the kind of life I want for me when I am old.

*   *   *

I think that when I gave up the questions, I missed many of the connections in the pasts of the Fifteen. But I learned so much about the quality of their lives in the present, and the interviews were so rich, that despite what I missed in their lives, I found so much in my own.

I discovered a new way of looking at retirement. I had always equated retirement with inactivity, and the thought of being inactive when I retired frightened me. As my wife once pointed out to me, I define myself by activity. Our garden is a yard that needs pruning and weeding, not a place where I can sit in the shade and read a book or watch birds. When I run out of things to do at home or at the office, I feel restless. I have always been afraid of not having a regular job to perform and a place to go five mornings a week. How relieved I was when the mandatory age for retirement was raised from 65 to 70! I could stay on the job for five more years!

Somewhere during the interviews something must have clicked, because I began to hear myself making different noises . . . like "Forty years of getting up at 6:15 A.M. is enough!" and "Wouldn't it be fun to work part-time in a hardware store?" I began to think of retirement as a time to do the things I *wanted* to, not *should* do . . . a time, not for inactivity, but for different kinds of activities . . . fun jobs, new hobbies, or maybe a whole new career. Gradually, the idea of retirement has changed from scary to pleasant. And now, instead of wondering whether to keep working till I'm 70, I'm starting to count down the months until I can retire, not at 65, but at 62! I may decide, when I get there, to put in more time at my job, but it will be the enjoyment of the job, not the fear of being without it, that will decide.

I also discovered that I was no longer uncomfortable about telling others about my fears of aging and dying . . . something I had rarely done before. I was constantly afraid of being laughed at for admitting to the fears. Any talks my wife and I had about death were always in the most oblique terms, like "community property" and "insurance beneficiaries." My discomfort got in the way of deeper discussions.

When I began interviewing, it was hard for me to ask people whom I didn't know, and who were probably much closer to dying than I was, whether they were afraid of death. I thought it would be hard for *them* to talk about it. My naivete was incredible. Not a single one had any difficulty discussing it! No one looked forward to dying, but no one feared it. Their concerns are for how, rather than when, they will die; they do not want lingering deaths any more than I do.

A turning point for me was hearing Elaine describe her vision of the recycling process that she saw in the tides of San Francisco Bay. Jeremiah Coulson said almost the same thing, and Liz Farrell told me "Why, we start dying the day we're born," but Elaine's words had a different impact. I know it was different because only a night or two after our interview, my wife and I had an easy, intimate talk about funerals, the quality of one of our lives after the other died, remarriage . . . the very topics I had previously swept under the rug. It was a loving talk, and it was one of the high points of the entire project.

The most gratifying moment followed a few days later while I was mulling over our talk. I was pleased as much with my readiness to open up and discuss death as I was with the content of the talk. At the same time, I felt sad . . . sad that in another 10 or 20 years I'd be leaving behind my wife and two sons whom I love, as well as some yet undefined, unfinished projects. That's when it hit me . . . while I was thinking about growing old and dying, I was no longer focusing on the naked light bulb in the SRO hotel. I was sad, not afraid! I felt so light-hearted with the discovery that I actually felt glad that I was feeling sad, and I kept repeating to myself, "I'm sad, not afraid . . . sad, not afraid. . . ."

*   *   *

Friends who have known that I was working on a book have asked me what it was about. My usual answer has been that it's a book about older people I interviewed, but written for people my age. It's still true . . . the focus is on those 15 people . . . but the book is also about how I grew by listening to them.

October, 1979

James Maas lives in Berkeley, California. He is married and has two sons. Formerly a businessman, he is now a civil servant by day, and a lecturer in Anthropology at the University of San Francisco by night. He holds Master's degrees in Anthropology and in Public Health, and a Doctorate in Social Gerontology.